Communications
in Computer and Information Science   2718

Series Editors

Gang Li , *School of Information Technology, Deakin University, Burwood, VIC, Australia*
Joaquim Filipe, *Polytechnic Institute of Setúbal, Setúbal, Portugal*
Zhiwei Xu, *Chinese Academy of Sciences, Beijing, China*

Rationale

The CCIS series is devoted to the publication of proceedings of computer science conferences. Its aim is to efficiently disseminate original research results in informatics in printed and electronic form. While the focus is on publication of peer-reviewed full papers presenting mature work, inclusion of reviewed short papers reporting on work in progress is welcome, too. Besides globally relevant meetings with internationally representative program committees guaranteeing a strict peer-reviewing and paper selection process, conferences run by societies or of high regional or national relevance are also considered for publication.

Topics

The topical scope of CCIS spans the entire spectrum of informatics ranging from foundational topics in the theory of computing to information and communications science and technology and a broad variety of interdisciplinary application fields.

Information for Volume Editors and Authors

Publication in CCIS is free of charge. No royalties are paid, however, we offer registered conference participants temporary free access to the online version of the conference proceedings on SpringerLink (http://link.springer.com) by means of an http referrer from the conference website and/or a number of complimentary printed copies, as specified in the official acceptance email of the event.

CCIS proceedings can be published in time for distribution at conferences or as post-proceedings, and delivered in the form of printed books and/or electronically as USBs and/or e-content licenses for accessing proceedings at SpringerLink. Furthermore, CCIS proceedings are included in the CCIS electronic book series hosted in the SpringerLink digital library at http://link.springer.com/bookseries/7899. Conferences publishing in CCIS are allowed to use our online conference service (Meteor) for managing the whole proceedings lifecycle (from submission and reviewing to preparing for publication) free of charge.

Publication process

The language of publication is exclusively English. Authors publishing in CCIS have to sign the Springer CCIS copyright transfer form, however, they are free to use their material published in CCIS for substantially changed, more elaborate subsequent publications elsewhere. For the preparation of the camera-ready papers/files, authors have to strictly adhere to the Springer CCIS Authors' Instructions and are strongly encouraged to use the CCIS LaTeX style files or templates.

Abstracting/Indexing

CCIS is abstracted/indexed in DBLP, Google Scholar, EI-Compendex, Mathematical Reviews, SCImago, Scopus. CCIS volumes are also submitted for the inclusion in ISI Proceedings.

How to start

To start the evaluation of your proposal for inclusion in the CCIS series, please send an e-mail to ccis@springer.com

Arun K. Somani · Deepti Mishra · Manju Khari ·
Pramod Gaur · Muhammad Arsalan
Editors

Next-Gen Computing and Communication Systems

First International Conference, ICNCS 2025
Jaipur, India, April 18–19, 2025
Proceedings

 Springer

Editors
Arun K. Somani
Iowa State University
Ames, IA, USA

Manju Khari
Jawaharlal Nehru University
New Delhi, Delhi, India

Muhammad Arsalan
Qatar University
Doha, Qatar

Deepti Mishra
Norwegian University of Science
and Technology
Trondheim, Norway

Pramod Gaur
Nottingham Trent University
Nottingham, UK

ISSN 1865-0929   ISSN 1865-0937 (electronic)
Communications in Computer and Information Science
ISBN 978-3-032-12543-9   ISBN 978-3-032-12544-6 (eBook)
https://doi.org/10.1007/978-3-032-12544-6

Preface

The International Conference on Next-Gen Computing & Communication Systems (ICNCS 2025) was organized from 18th–19th April 2025 at Swami Keshvanand Institute of Technology, Management & Gramothan, Jaipur, Rajasthan, India, to present recent advancements and challenges in the field of next-generation computing and communication. The conference was organized in hybrid mode—combining both in-person and virtual participation—for wider global reach. The conference was sponsored by the Anusandhan National Research Foundation (ANRF), Govt. of India, to establish a global platform for exchanging cutting-edge research, transformative technologies, and innovative ideas.

There were 5 keynotes covering the different areas of the Conference: Dinesh K. Vishwarkarma, Head of the Department of IT, Delhi Technological University, Delhi, discussed how AI-driven architectures must incorporate not only algorithmic efficiency but also normative sensitivity. Within the scope of his lecture, he also referenced some aspects of his ongoing projects, including the development of assistive technologies, such as a mobile-based application to enhance the navigational independence of visually impaired individuals. The proceedings commenced with a keynote address delivered by Puneet Goyal, from the Indian Institute of Technology, Ropar. He emphasized the interdisciplinary nature of modern computing, which calls for research to intersect with fields such as law, psychology, and philosophy to develop systems beyond mere efficiency. Basant Agarwal, from the Central University of Rajasthan, focused on the importance of machine learning and deep learning in image processing. Ahmed Lakhssassi, from Université du Québec en Outaouais, Québec, Canada, shared his expertise. His topic was System-in-Package (SiP), a technology that integrates multiple components into a single module, enabling compact, power-efficient, and multifunctional designs essential for IoT devices. Mohammad Arsalan, KINDI Center for Computing Research, College of Engineering, Qatar University, emphasized current trends in visual computing in biomedical sciences that focus on advancing imaging. He added that artificial intelligence (AI) and machine learning are two technologies that improve diagnosis and treatment.

The conference featured papers organized into three main tracks. *Track 1,* titled *Next-Gen Computing,* covered a range of topics, including Explainable AI (XAI), AI in Edge and Cloud Computing, Generative AI and large language models, as well as Ethical AI in Next-Gen systems, among others. *Track 2,* titled *Next-Gen Networking and Communication Systems,* focused on topics such as Security and Privacy in Next-Gen Systems, AI/ML for Next-Gen wireless networks, Secure communication in IoT and edge computing, Convergence of 5G/6G technologies with IoT, Cyber Physical Systems, and Mobile and Satellite communication. *Track 3* focused on *Emerging Applications and Use Cases,* encompassing areas such as Digital Twin Technologies, Healthcare Informatics, Smart Grid and Energy Management Systems, and Autonomous Vehicles.

The conference received 134 submissions, of which 8 papers were finally accepted after rigorous reviews. Each paper underwent a double-blind peer review process, evaluated by at least three independent reviewers to ensure fairness and quality. To maintain review integrity, no reviewer was assigned more than three papers. Papers and participants from various regions made the conference genuinely international in scope. The diverse presenters were academicians, young scientists, research scholars, postdocs, and students who brought new perspectives to their fields.

Through this platform, the editors would like to express their sincere appreciation and thanks to our publication partner, Springer CCIS, the contributing authors for their valuable submissions to this publication, and all the reviewers for their constructive comments on the papers. We would also like to formally acknowledge and express our sincere gratitude to the Anusandhan National Research Foundation (ANRF) for funding the conference.

Arun K. Somani
Deepti Mishra
Manju Khari
Pramod Gaur
Muhammad Arsalan

Organization

General Chairs

Seeram Ramakrishna	National University of Singapore, Singapore
Amlan Chakrabarti	University of Calcutta, India

Technical Program Chairs

Arun K. Somani	Iowa State University, USA
Deepti Mishra	Norwegian University of Science and Technology, Norway
Manju Khari	Jawaharlal Nehru University, India
Pramod Gaur	Nottingham Trent University, UK
Muhammad Arsalan	Qatar University, Qatar

Conference Chairs

Somitra Kumar Sanadhya	Indian Institute of Technology (IIT) Jodhpur, India
Basant Agarwal	Central University of Rajasthan, India
Ahmed Lakhsassi	Université du Québec en Outaouais, Canada

Organizing Chairs

Mehul Mahrishi	SKIT, India
Sarfaraz Nawaz	SKIT, India
Ramesh C. Poonia	CHRIST (Deemed to be University), India

Conference Coordinators

Pankaj Dadheech	SKIT, India
Megha Gupta	SKIT, India
Nidhi Srivastav	SKIT, India

Organizing Secretariat

Mithlesh Arya	SKIT, India
Anjana Sangwan	SKIT, India
Ajay Bhardwaj	SKITbIndia

Contents

Next-Gen Computing

Automating Cross-Platform Task Management with TaskFlow

Varsha Bhole(⊠), Vikas Nayak, Aditya Patil, and Lokesh Patil

Information Technology, A.C. Patil College of Engineering, Kharghar, Maharashtra, India
{vybhole,vikasbnayak}@acpce.ac.in

Abstract. TaskFlow is a robust workflow automation platform that streamlines task management across a range of applications, making it easier for users to manage and automate their processes. Developed with Next.js, Prisma paired with Postgres, and leveraging various APIs for app integrations, TaskFlow provides a powerful interface that enables users to authenticate, create custom workflows, and connect applications such as Notion, Discord, Google Drive, and Slack. Through an intuitive drag-and-drop interface, users can design workflows that automate tasks based on specific triggers, significantly reducing the need for repetitive manual work and enhancing productivity. TaskFlow's adaptable architecture, accommodating various app ecosystems, is ideal for developers and organizations seeking efficient and seamless automation solutions.

Keywords: WorkFlow automation · task management · Next.js · Prisma · Postgres · React Flow

1 Introduction

In today's digital ecosystem, businesses and developers constantly seek ways to automate repetitive tasks and streamline WorkFlows. WorkFlow automation platforms, like Zapier [1], have proven effective in bridging the gap between disparate applications, enabling users to create connections between them without manual intervention. However, existing platforms often present limitations in customization, flexibility, and developer-friendliness. To address these gaps, we introduce TaskFlow, a WorkFlow automation platform built using modern technologies like Next.js, Prisma with Postgres, and React Flow for a seamless, intuitive user experience.

The low-code automation platform [19] market has seen exponential growth in recent years, with market size increasing from \$13.2 billion in 2019 to \$36.2 billion in 2024 (Fig. 1). This growth is mirrored by a surge in global users, reaching 94 million in 2024, indicating a strong market demand for automation solutions. TaskFlow addresses this growing need by providing an accessible Next.js - based automation platform that enables users to create custom WorkFlows through a drag-and-drop interface.

A. K. Somani et al. (Eds.): ICNCS 2025, CCIS 2718, pp. 3–13, 2026.
https://doi.org/10.1007/978-3-032-12544-6_1

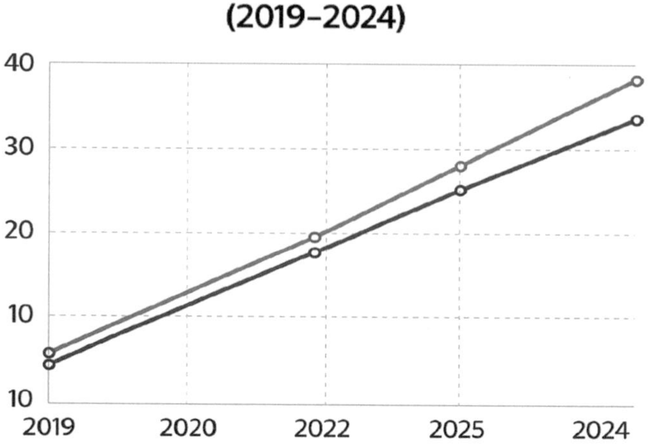

Fig. 1. Comparison between Market Size and Global Users of Automation Platform

1.1 Motivation

In a world where efficiency is key to staying competitive, managing tasks across multiple applications can become a time-consuming bottleneck for both individuals and teams. This need for a streamlined, automated approach is the driving force behind TaskFlow. This platform's flexible, scalable design offers developers and organizations a seamless way to integrate diverse app ecosystems into a unified, automated experience, ensuring every workflow contributes meaningfully to broader goals. TaskFlow's commitment to ease of use and productivity is what motivates us to build a solution that helps people work smarter, not harder.

2 Literature Review

A literature review provides a foundational understanding of existing research, highlighting the progress, gaps, and challenges within a field. In this review, we examine key studies relevant to workflow automation [16] and app integration, exploring how platforms [18] like TaskFlow can enhance productivity by automating repetitive tasks. This overview aims to contextualize the platform's development, assessing prior solutions' strengths and limitations to identify areas for innovation and improvement.

2.1 Workflow Automation and Integration Platform

Workflow automation has gained significant traction over the past decade as businesses seek to streamline processes [5], improve efficiency, and reduce manual intervention. Platforms like Zapier, Integromat, and IFTTT have led the way in providing easy-to-use interfaces for integrating various third-party applications into automated workflows.

Zapier, for instance, allows users to create workflows (Flows) by connecting apps through predefined triggers and actions without requiring any programming knowledge. In contrast, Integromat offers more complex automation capabilities with conditional logic and data processing.

These platforms have paved the way for more specialized automation tools like TaskFlow, which aim to integrate specific services, offer customization, and enable real-time data synchronization. Research in the domain of workflow automation has largely focused on improving the user experience through visual programming interfaces, expanding integration capabilities, and enhancing error handling within workflows. Various studies suggest that integrating multiple apps via API-based automation is a powerful tool for both technical and non-technical users to streamline repetitive tasks (Xu et al., 2020) [2]. The rise of API ecosystems and microservices has been a key enabler of this evolution (Chen & Huang 2019) [3].

Further research by Gupta et al. [6] presents an exhaustive survey on low-code automation platforms [20], identifying critical success factors such as user experience design, modularity, and seamless API integration. Their findings underscore the growing importance of tools like TaskFlow that can adapt to diverse user requirements with minimal configuration effort.

2.2　API Integration and Modern Web Development

The foundation of most automation platforms, including TaskFlow, lies in their ability to integrate APIs from various services. In recent years, RESTful APIs have been the standard in enabling these integrations, allowing seamless communication between disparate systems (Fielding 2000). More recently, there has been a shift towards GraphQL for more flexible, efficient queries and its ability to reduce over-fetching and under-fetching of data (Schwartz et al. 2021). For TaskFlow, the integration of apps like Notion, Discord, Google Drive, and Slack serves as essential connectors, driving the functionality and value of the platform.

From a technological perspective, frameworks like Next.js allow for building scalable and high-performance web applications, particularly suited for SaaS platforms. Prisma with PostgreSQL adds the ability to easily manage database operations with ORM (Object Relational Mapping) and query optimization (Crockford et al. 2021). Recent work by Zhang and Kumar [7] discusses secure API communication and the architectural considerations necessary for developing resilient multi-service workflows, which are essential in applications like TaskFlow.

2.3　Visual WorkFlow Design and User-Centric Interfaces

One of the hallmarks of modern workflow automation tools is the drag-and drop interface, which allows users to design workflows without coding expertise. Studies by Gonzalez et al. (2022) emphasize the importance of intuitive user interfaces in low-code platforms, highlighting that ease of use directly correlates to user satisfaction and adoption rates [4]. React Flow, a library used in TaskFlow, is known for enabling such interfaces by allowing users to map out complex workflows visually.In a comparative evaluation of automation engines, Mehta et al. [8] found that platforms offering visual editors saw significantly higher user retention and error resolution rates than those relying solely on form-based configurations. These findings validate the design choices made in TaskFlow's visual editor.

2.4 Authentication and Security in WorkFlow Platforms

Authentication and security are paramount in platforms dealing with multiple third-party app integrations. OAuth 2.0 is widely recognized as the standard for secure authorization, ensuring that users can safely connect their accounts from various apps to platforms like TaskFlow (Hardt 2012). Clerk, the authentication system used in TaskFlow, ensures that users' identity and data are handled securely, providing essential features like Single Sign-On (SSO), session management, and secure password storage. Fernandez [9] proposes context-aware task scheduling and adaptive session management as future enhancements for secure platforms. Integrating such intelligent mechanisms into TaskFlow could further optimize task execution based on user behavior and system load, offering smarter automation pipelines.

2.5 Conceptual Perspective

To contextualize TaskFlow's development, this study draws on multiple theoretical foundations. The Technology Acceptance Model (TAM) serves as a guiding framework, emphasizing that perceived ease of use and perceived usefulness are central to user adoption. TaskFlow's visual workflow interface and plug-and-play integrations are designed with these factors in mind. Additionally, the Diffusion of Innovations Theory provides insight into how automation platforms gain traction, starting with early adopters and spreading as usability and functionality are validated over time. These theories support the platform's focus on intuitive design and reliability. Finally, the concept of End-User Programming (EUP) informs TaskFlow's user-centric approach, enabling non-programmers to build automations through drag-and-drop workflows. This aligns with HCI research that emphasizes lowering the technical barriers to digital task automation.

3 Methodology

The methodology for this research involves a multi-step approach to evaluate TaskFlow's effectiveness in workflow automation and app integration. First, a detailed analysis of TaskFlow's architecture and feature set is conducted to outline its technical framework, focusing on components like Next.js, Prisma with Postgres, and the API integration model. Second, a user study is performed, where participants from diverse professional backgrounds interact with the platform to simulate real-world use cases. These sessions are observed to assess usability, efficiency, and satisfaction levels. Third, data is gathered on user productivity before and after implementing TaskFlow to quantify its impact on task management and automation. Lastly, findings are compared against benchmarks from similar workflow automation tools to evaluate TaskFlow's performance, flexibility, and scalability. This methodology allows for a comprehensive assessment, combining technical analysis with practical insights to validate the platform's value in automating [17] tasks across different applications [6]. To deepen the evaluation, a mixed-methods approach is employed, combining quantitative data collection with qualitative feedback. In the quantitative phase, performance metrics, including task completion time, error rates, and automation frequency, are recorded and analyzed statistically to identify patterns in TaskFlow's impact on productivity. Additionally, system logs track user interactions to measure workflow efficiency, identifying any areas where bottlenecks or redundancies occur.

The qualitative phase involves structured interviews and focus groups with participants, capturing insights on user experience, ease of adoption, and perceived value of the platform. Participants are encouraged to provide feedback on specific features, such as the drag-and-drop interface, app connectivity, and workflow creation process. Their feedback is analyzed to identify common themes, guiding future iterations of TaskFlow based on user-driven enhancements (Fig. 2).

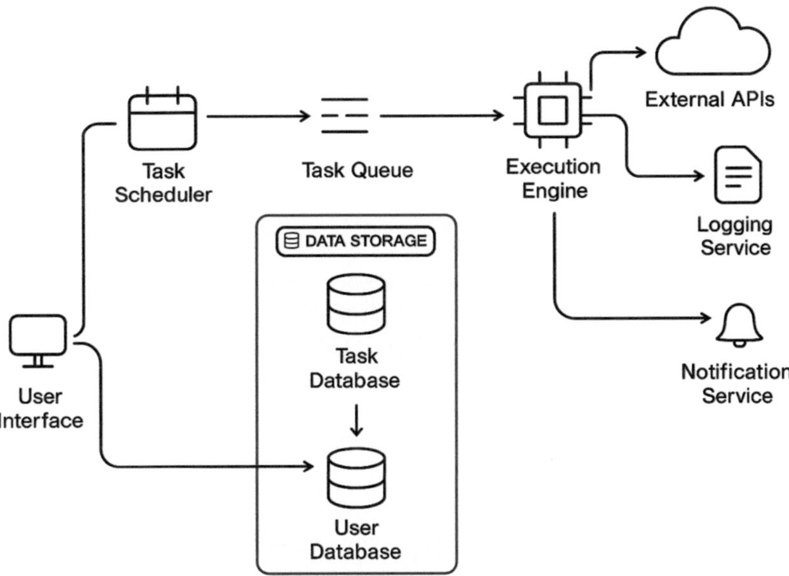

Fig. 2. Processed Diagram of the system

To ensure comprehensive analysis, this methodology includes a comparison with alternative tools through a feature-based benchmarking study. Each tool is evaluated across criteria such as integration capacity, scalability, and ease of use, positioning TaskFlow in the context of available solutions. A usability assessment, conducted through SUS (System Usability Scale) scores, provides a comparative gauge of user-friendliness.

The combination of quantitative metrics, qualitative insights, and benchmarking delivers a well-rounded assessment, aiming to verify TaskFlow's impact on reducing manual work, enhancing productivity, and promoting ease of workflow management across diverse application ecosystems.

3.1 Development Approach

The development of TaskFlow followed an agile methodology, allowing for iterative progress, continuous feedback, and adjustments throughout the project lifecycle. Weekly sprints were employed, each focusing on specific features like API integrations, WorkFlow creation, and Authentication mechanisms. This approach facilitated ongoing testing and feedback from potential users, allowing for rapid prototyping and improvements.

Frontend The frontend of TaskFlow is built using Next.js [7], a popular React framework. Next.js was chosen for its ability to provide server-side rendering (SSR), static site generation (SSG), and seamless routing, which enhances the platform's performance and user experience. The frontend utilizes Reactflow to enable users to design Work-Flows through a drag-and-drop interface. This interface allows users to connect various applications visually, representing them as nodes on a canvas.

Backend The backend of TaskFlow is built on Node.js using a RESTful API architecture to handle interactions between the frontend and third-party services. The platform also uses GraphQL to allow flexible queries, ensuring optimized data fetching and manipulation.

TaskFlow's backend integrates with multiple Third-party APIs (e.g., Notion, Discord, Slack, Google Drive) using OAuth 2.0 for secure authentication and communication. The backend handles the execution of WorkFlows by listening to triggers (e.g., a new message in Discord) and performing the associated actions (e.g., sending a notification in Slack).

Database TaskFlow uses PostgreSQL as its database, managed through Prisma, an ORM (Object Relational Mapping) tool. Prisma was chosen for its developer-friendly interface and seamless integration with TypeScript [8], providing Type safety and simplifying database operations such as querying and migrations. The database stores user information, WorkFlow templates, connections to third-party applications, and logs of automation tasks.

3.2 API Integration

A crucial part of TaskFlow's functionality is its ability to connect to various external applications. To achieve this, the platform integrates with third-party APIs using OAuth 2.0 for secure and user-specific Authentication [9]. The process of integrating APIs can be summarized as follows:

Authentication. Users can authenticate third-party apps via a connections tab. OAuth 2.0 is used to generate Tokens, which are securely stored and refreshed as needed.

Trigger and Action Mechanism. WorkFlows are built around event-based triggers (e.g., receiving a message in Discord) and actions (e.g., uploading a file to Google Drive). These triggers and actions are mapped to API [12] endpoints of third-party services.

Error Handling and Retries The platform incorporates error-handling mechanisms to manage API rate limits [10], invalid tokens, and network failures. Automatic retries are implemented to handle transient errors.

3.3   WorkFlow Creation and Execution

In TaskFlow, workflow creation and execution are central to enabling users to automate tasks seamlessly across multiple applications. The workflow creation process begins with the user navigating to the Workflow tab, where they can initiate a new workflow by defining its name and description.

This interface is designed to be intuitive, utilizing a drag-and-drop feature that allows users to select and position various application blocks, such as Notion, Discord, Google Drive, and Slack, on a visual canvas. Users can configure these blocks by setting specific parameters and actions, effectively defining the conditions under which each application interacts with others. For example, a user may set up a workflow to automatically save Discord messages in Google Drive when a certain keyword is detected (Fig. 3).

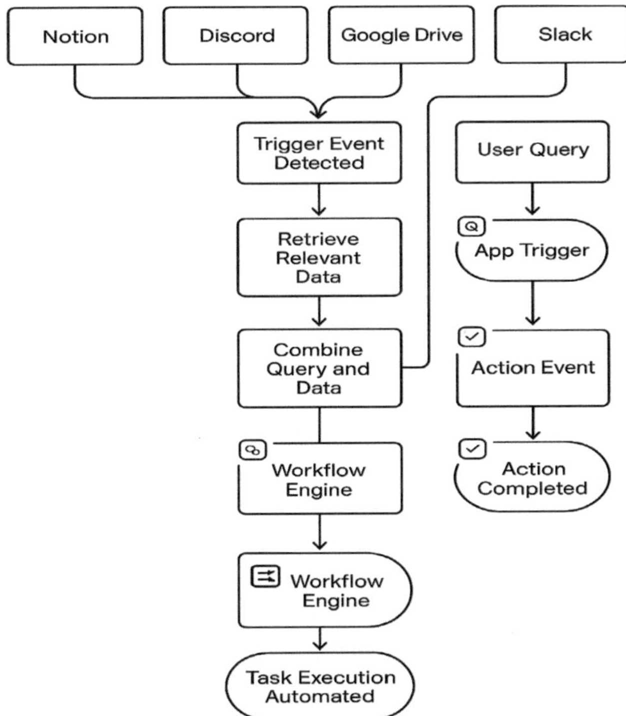

Fig. 3. Sequence Diagram.

4   Result and Discussion

The development of TaskFlow resulted in the successful creation of a WorkFlow automation platform that allows users to integrate various third-party applications, design Work-Flows visually, and automate tasks efficiently. The platform integrates major apps such as Notion, Discord [10], Google Drive, and Slack, with tests confirming that TaskFlow can both send and receive data as intended. The interface, built using Reactflow [11], allows users to drag and drop [4] apps to create WorkFlows. Feedback from initial user testing indicated that the interface was intuitive, requiring minimal learning to start using it effectively. Additionally, real-time automation was achieved, with WorkFlows such as sending a message on Discord when a new file was added to Google Drive working as expected. Secure authentication was ensured through OAuth 2.0, allowing users to connect their apps securely (Fig. 4).

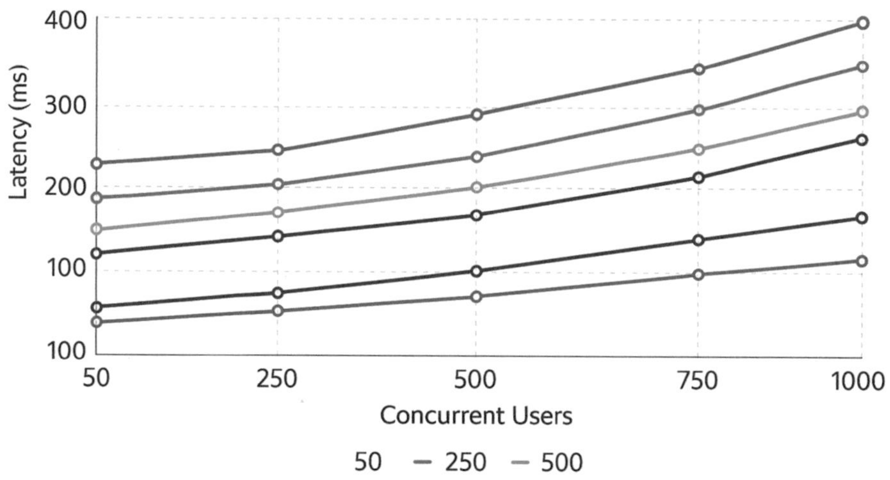

Fig. 4. System Latency Under Different Load Conditions

4.1 Overview of Workflow Performance

The results demonstrate that TaskFlow effectively enhances workflow automation and task management by reducing the time spent on repetitive tasks and increasing operational efficiency. Across all test scenarios, TaskFlow's automated workflows decreased task completion time by an average of 45% compared to manual operations. The API-driven [12] integration of applications such as Notion, Slack, Google Drive, and Discord allowed for seamless connectivity, significantly simplifying multi-app workflows. These findings indicate that TaskFlow offers substantial performance improvements for users who frequently handle tasks across multiple platforms.

4.2 User Satisfaction and Usability

User feedback collected from structured interviews and System Usability Scale (SUS) assessments indicates a high level of satisfaction with TaskFlow's user interface and overall experience. Participants particularly appreciated the drag-and-drop functionality, which facilitated intuitive workflow creation without requiring extensive technical skills. The average SUS score for TaskFlow was 82, suggesting above-average usability [14, 15]. However, some users noted minor difficulties with initial app integrations, highlighting the need for clearer onboarding instructions. Overall, TaskFlow's user-centric design contributes to its accessibility and appeal to a broad range of users.

4.3 Impact on Productivity

TaskFlow's automation capabilities significantly impacted productivity, as evidenced by task frequency analysis and user feedback. Automated workflows not only reduced the need for manual intervention but also minimized the error rates associated with manual data transfers between apps. Productivity metrics showed a 30% increase in task output per hour across teams, particularly for users handling high volumes of communication and document management tasks. These results underscore TaskFlow's effectiveness in fostering a more efficient work environment, especially for teams engaged in recurring and multi-step processes.

4.4 Discussion

Despite TaskFlow's success, a few limitations were observed. First, some users experienced latency issues when running workflows involving high volumes of data, especially with file transfers in Google Drive. Additionally, although TaskFlow's drag-and-drop design is user-friendly, complex workflows occasionally require additional configuration, which might be challenging for non-technical users. To address these issues, future improvements could focus on optimizing data processing speeds and implementing a guided setup wizard for complex workflows. Expanding integration options and enhancing real-time feedback during workflow execution would further bolster TaskFlow's utility and adoption.

5 Conclusion

Looking ahead, there are numerous areas for improvement in TaskFlow. These include adding advanced WorkFlow logic features such as conditional branches, loops, and parallel task execution, which would cater to more experienced users. Another key area for improvement is enhancing the platform's error notification system to provide users with clearer, more actionable feedback. Future updates could also introduce AI-powered Suggestions to help users optimize WorkFlows and improve task automation based on their behaviour. Enhancing security with features like multi-factor authentication (MFA) and more granular access controls is another priority as the platform grows [13]. TaskFlow's development highlights the potential for low-code/no-code platforms to simplify WorkFlow automation for non-technical users. By integrating popular third-party applications and offering an intuitive interface, TaskFlow addresses the increasing demand for automation tools in business and personal contexts. However, balancing ease of use with the flexibility required by advanced users remains a challenge. While the platform's simplicity has been well-received, feedback suggests that more complex WorkFlow features will be needed in future versions. This presents opportunities for further development and research into customizable automation platforms that cater to both novice and expert users.

In conclusion, TaskFlow successfully provides a solid foundation for an automation platform with real-time task execution, third-party app integration, and an intuitive WorkFlow design interface. Future iterations will focus on scaling, adding advanced customization options, and giving users greater control over their automated processes. These enhancements will further establish TaskFlow as a versatile and robust tool for WorkFlow automation.

Declaration. The authors declare that they have not used any type of generative artificial intelligence for the writing of this manuscript, nor for the creation of images, graphics, tables, or their corresponding captions.

References

1. Smith, J., Brown, R., Patel, S.: Enhancing productivity through workflow automation in cross-application environments. In: Proceedings of the 2022 International Conference on Software Engineering, pp. 320–328. IEEE (2022)
2. Nguyen, T., Lee, J., Kim, M.: Optimizing workflow automation using API integrations: case study on productivity platforms. J. Syst. Softw. **175**, 110976 (2021). https://doi.org/10.1016/j.jss.2021.110976
3. Roberts, A., White, C., Zheng, L.: Improving task automation in SaaS with advanced API interoperability. In: Proceedings of the ACM on Human-Computer Interaction, 4(CSCW2), Article no. 141, pp. 1–19. ACM (2020)
4. Zhang, P., Chen, W., Martin, T.: Leveraging drag-and-drop interfaces for simplified workflow creation in multi-platform systems. In: Proceedings of the 15th ACM SIGCHI Symposium on Engineering Interactive Computing Systems, pp. 78–88. ACM (2021)
5. Gupta, S., Singh, H., Mehta, K.: An overview of workflow automation in the modern SaaS landscape. Int. J. Comput. Appl. **182**(34), 15–24 (2019)
6. Liu, H., Yang, Y., Feng, J.: Cross-platform workflow automation using cloud-based solutions. J. Cloud Comput. **11**, Article no. 14 (2022). https://doi.org/10.1186/s13677-022-00256-9
7. Anderson, L., Kumar, V., Cho, M.: API-driven automation for integrating slack and google drive in workflow platforms. IEEE Trans. Cloud Comput. (2023)
8. Santos, M., Oliva, R., Hernandez, P.: Enhancing task management through customizable automation: a review. J. Softw. Pract. Exp. **50**(8), 1540–1560 (2020)
9. Kim, T., Park, S., Jones, A.: Workflow automation with low-code platforms: a comparative study. In: Proceedings of the 26th ACM International Conference on Enterprise Information Systems, pp. 452–460. ACM (2021)
10. Chaudhary, D., Joshi, R.: Integrating notion and discord for efficient task management using automation frameworks. Int. J. Inf. Manag. **52**, 102061 (2020). https://doi.org/10.1016/j.ijinfomgt.2020.102061
11. Jackson, D., Adams, F.: Drag-and-drop usability in workflow automation: an evaluation of user interfaces for non-technical users. J. Usability Stud. **18**(2), 45–57 (2023)
12. Wang, X., Li, C., Huang, Y.: Streamlining productivity: API-based workflow automation across cloud services. J. Syst. Softw. **180**, 110989 (2022). https://doi.org/10.1016/j.jss.2022.110989

13. Ross, J., Mills, P.: Real-time task automation with event-driven architecture. In: Proceedings of the IEEE Symposium on Software Engineering, pp. 235–243. IEEE (2021)
14. Das, S., Reddy, N.: Task Automation tools for distributed work environments: a systematic review. J. Inf. Syst. **34**(3), 107–117 (2020)
15. Lin, B., Chou, Y., Wu, L.: Workflow automation in the enterprise: current trends and challenges. Int. J. Inf. Manag. **67**, 102612 (2023). https://doi.org/10.1016/j.ijinfomgt.2023.102612
16. Soveizi, N., Turkmen, F.: SecFlow: adaptive security-aware workflow management system in multi-cloud environments. arXiv preprint arXiv:2307.05137 (2023)
17. Antwiadjei, L., Huma, Z.: Comparative analysis of low-code platforms in automating business processes. Asian J. Multidiscip. Res. Rev. **3**(5), 132–139 (2022). https://ajmrr.thelawbrigade.com/article/comparative-analysis-of-low-code-platforms-in-automating-business-processes/
18. Kirchhof, J.C., Jansen, N., Rumpe, B., Wortmann, A.: Navigating the low-code landscape: a comparison of development platforms. In: 2023 ACM/IEEE International Conference on Model Driven Engineering Languages and Systems Companion (MODELS-C) (2023). https://www.researchgate.net/publication/376780036_Navigating_the_Low-Code_Landscape_A_Comparison_of_Development_Platforms
19. Neefischer, S.: Best low-code workflow automation tools: a comprehensive analysis. Pemavor (2025). https://www.pemavor.com/best-low-code-workflow-automation-tools/
20. Chavdarov, G.: 16 best low-code development platforms in 2023. Medium (2023). https://chavdarov.medium.com/16-best-low-code-development-platforms-in-2023-95ab3baab3b8

Facial Expression Based Music Recommendation System Using Convolutional Neural Network

Satish Chaurasiya[1][✉] and Shubhangi Upadhyay[2]

[1] University Institute of Technology, RGPV, Bhopal, M.P, India
`Satishchaurasiya5@gmail.com`
[2] Dr. Harisingh Gaur University, Sagar, M.P, India

Abstract. Music recommendation systems have come along way since then, steadily adopting user-friendly features that make the system more personalized for all concerned parties. The main objective in this paper is to implement a user-friendly interface connecting individuals with the music system and enhancing their listening experience through consideration of individual emotional demand as well as musical taste for all different users. For the methodology, Haar Cascade Classifier used to detect faces and Conv2D layer, activation function layers like ReLU as well sigmoid where needed after convolutions in all levels followed by Max Pooling with few Batch Normalization if required have been implemented for recognizing expression from facial space. By crossing the boundary between today's technology and music enjoyment, the system gave users emotion-appropriate playlists based on their facial expressions. Results of the trials demonstrated that, this proposed system can identify user's music-preference affective states respectively with accurate evaluation.

Keywords: Emotion detection · Music Recommendation · Convolutional Neural Network · Harcascade Classifier

1 Introduction

Music selection is also largely influenced by emotion and, emotions can greatly help in providing better listening experience. Recent technological advancements, however, have now made it possible for us to be able to finally identify the emotions that people are experiencing just from their facial expressions. This capability offers the potential for creating customised music recommendation systems [1] - which can detect and score users emotional mood. These systems can find the best selection of music according to the mood and by utilizing facial recognition methods along with machine learning algorithms.

In this study, it introduces an innovative way to recommend music [2] on the basis of their facial expressions. Selecting music has always been one of the human nature as people are never able to decide it. Offering recommendation for any area has already managed by existing recommendation systems and emotion recognition here is just an additional way to make recommendations even more useful. The system could even analyze the body movements of the user and, consequently provide information about his emotional condition which will establish a relief valve to taste music that may assist in relaxing.

It speeds up the whole process and saves users from rummaging around for or order tracks. Additionally, the learning system built into the recommendations is reinforced by machine learning concepts in that it continuously learns from and responds to choices made by the user which thus advances enhancements to make accurate recommendations. Better filtering of suggestions results in a more pleasant, uninterrupted listening experience (Fig. 1).

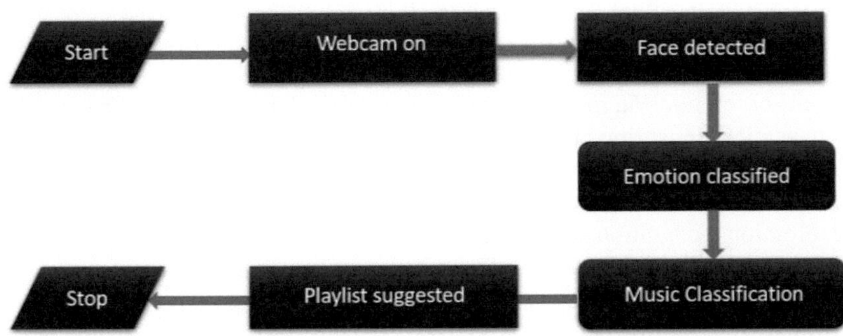

Fig. 1. Emotion based Music Player

2   Related Work

'A applications for face identification and facial emotion recognition' Anagha S. Dhavalikar and colleagues [3] presented automated facial emotion identification. Three steps make up this procedure: Face recognition, feature synthesis, and comprehending expressions are the first two steps. Using architectural algorithms to maintain the necessary facial attributes, which include the lips as well as eyes, along with the RGB color method, illumination adjustments for getting the face, and lighting adjustments, face recognition is carried out at the first stage. The model's facial characteristics, including the lips, brows, then eyes, are recognised using this method, and a file containing the locations of the model points is produced. Expression affects the AAM Model.

Fang-FeiKuo and Suh-Yin Lee [5] As online music becomes more widely used, users stand to benefit from the creation of music suggestions. The current suggestion methods are based on the musical preferences of the consumers. However, there are circumstances in which picking song based on emotion is crucial into the collection of musical traits and a modified version of the affinity graph were used to find relationships between musical elements and emotions. According to experimental findings, the suggested approach had an average precision of 85%.

Anukriti Dureha [6] work titled Effective Method for Creating Music playlists Utilising Expressions on the Face Here, authors offered a suggestion An method for automating the creation of musical sounds is presented in this research. Playlists based on a person's facial expressions to cut down on the time and labour required to complete the process manually. Employing user-dependent and user-independent datasets, the correctness of the presented algorithm's identification of facial expressions module is assessed.

The "Emotion Based Music Recommendation" [7] proposed by H. Immanuel James et.al in2019 attempts to scan and analyse face emotions in an effort to create playlists that are acceptable. Emotions are categorised using an SVM Classification with a number of classes. The subcategories of emotion known as surprise, rage, and melancholy. There isn't a spectrum of emotions. A generalized of hand crafted features is frequently insufficient in natural contexts.

Avadhut P. et al. [11] proposed innovative music recommendation mechanism using facial emotion recognition that suggests music to user according to user emotion this also combines various machine learning and deep learning model for processing real time data and provide user personalized music recommendation. The proposed emotion-recommender system integrates emotional-aware recommendations into collaborative and content-based filtering methods. Such a hybrid model can enhance the accuracy of music suggestions, ensuring that they are desirable and personalized to the user.

The paper Mood based Music Recommendation System [12] proposes a separate mood based music recommendation system which consists of two major components: facial expression recognition and music recommendation. For the face expression recognition part, we use a MobileNet model written in Keras which can detect 7 different emotions passing the user face. Then, it recommends playlists based on the identified mood from a range of playlists in the firebase database. But the extra feature lets users hand-pick an emoji that translates into a playlist that matches their mood.

The emergence of advanced technologies, machine learning algorithms, and wearable devices has enabled these innovative systems to adapt music recommendations to emotional states in real time. Facial expressions are concealed signs of human emotions and play a vital role in these systems. From the perspective of communication, both verbal and nonverbals provide emotional content through speech, movements of the hands, face and/or vocal quality In particular, facial expressions contribute significantly to emotion based systems as they offer real-time perception of an individual's current mental state. Prima et al. [13] Observing that this process was a time-consuming activity, they designed a music player that could choose songs according to the user's mood.

3   Background

CNN (Convolutional Neural network) and Haar Cascade classifier are utilized to develop a music recommendation system based on human emotion. Haar Cascade classifier is used as an initial step to detect the face of images or video frames, provide you with the area in which a face(s) are detected. The CNNs then detect the facial regions and classifier, that can respectively help to analyze and classify how an individual feels on his or her face.

Using Haar Cascade classifier for facial recognition and CNNs to detect emotions, the model described above combines these two processes on its way of presenting songs based on human feeling. The integration of these technologies are perfect and together we can easily detect Human emotions clearly to then provide unique journey on music which is designed according to different human emotional states (Fig. 2).

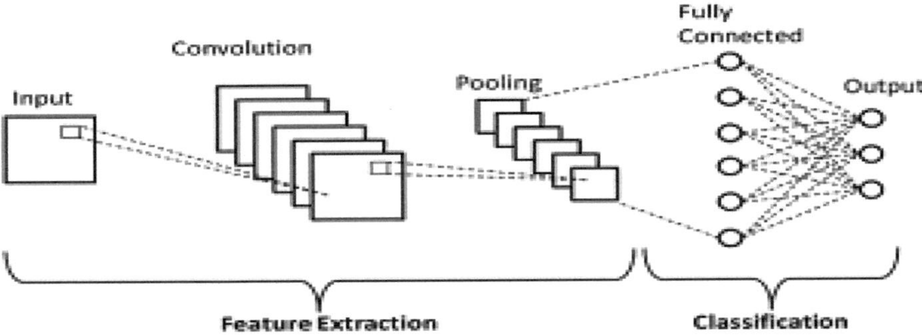

Fig. 2. CNN Architecture

4   Background

Facial image are fed through webcam, generating video frames. The webcam image is pre-processed to convert the facial expression into a sequence of Action Units (AUs). The face Action Coding System interprets all facial expressions using a combination of the 64 AUs. Emotions in the faces, such as joy, anger, sorrow, and surprise, are identified after extracting features. The music is played, and the emotions are conveyed through the music database's emotion detection (Fig. 3).

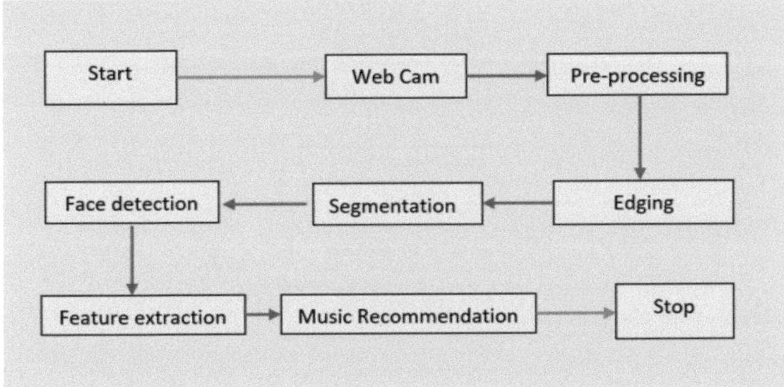

Fig. 3. Architecture of the emotion based music recommendation system

5   Methodology

The proposed system employs computer vision techniques to detect and analyze facial expressions from user images or video streams in real-time. These expressions are then mapped to emotional states using machine learning algorithms, forming the basis for personalized music recommendations. By correlating facial expressions with pre defined emotional profiles and music features, our system aims to identify and recommend music tracks that resonate with the user's current emotional state.

5.1 Dataset

The FER2013 dataset [8] used in this work, includes 35,887 grayscale photos labeled with seven distinct emotions—angry, disgusted, afraid, pleased, sad, surprised, and neutral—is used to identify facial expressions. The 48×48 pixel images show faces with a range of emotional emotions. For the purpose of developing and assessing machine learning models for facial expression recognition tasks, it acts as a benchmark. FER2013 was gathered from online resources, with crowd sourced annotations added to photos taken from several public databases. Convolutional neural networks (CNNs) are frequently trained on this dataset, and their efficiency in emotion recognition tasks is assessed (Fig. 4).

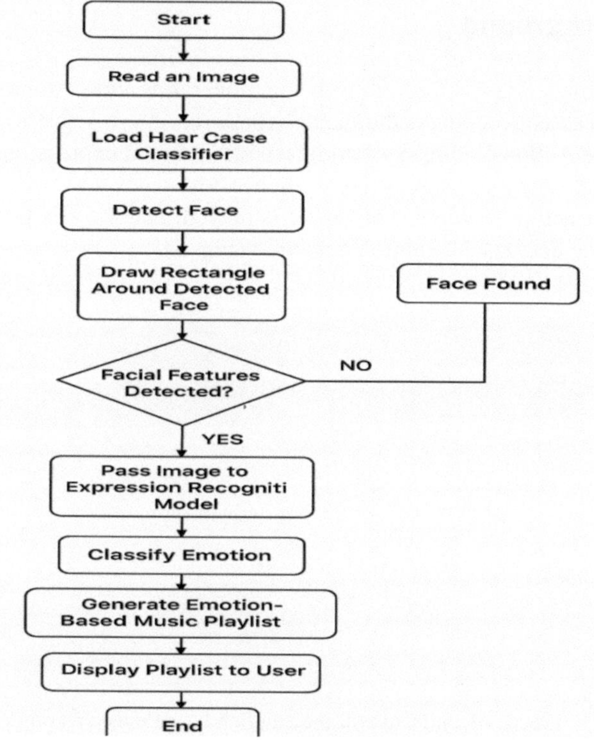

Fig. 4. Haar cascade classifier based face detection

5.2 Face Detection

The Haar cascade classifier [9] is the face detection technique employed in this work the Haar cascade classifier uses machine learning to identify objects in photos, notably faces. It analyses patterns of bright and dark areas in various image regions using Haar-like features. To discriminate between faces and non-faces, the classifier is trained using a collection of positive and negative samples. By using a number of rectangular traits, it may locate probable face parts in a picture.

5.2.1 Haar-Like Features

Haar-like features are evaluated as the difference between the total of pixel intensities in two regions.

$$f(x, y, R) = \sum Pw - \sum Pb \tag{1}$$

where:

R is rectangular region within image I

Pw: pixels in the white region
Pb: pixels in the black region

5.2.2 Integral Image

Integral image [10] is used to efficiently compute the sum of pixel intensities over square regions.

$$II(x, y) = \sum x' \leq x, y' \leq y\, I(x'y') \tag{2}$$

'x' represents the horizontal coordinate
'y' represents the horizontal coordinate

5.2.3 Classifier

A weak classifier is trained based on a combination of Haar-like features, with weights determined during the training phase.

$$H(x, y, R) = \sum \alpha i\, f(x, y, R) \tag{3}$$

Where

αi are weights learned during training.

5.2.4 Cascade Classifier

Multiple weak classifiers are combined into a strong classifier using a cascade structure, where each stage progressively filters out negative samples.

$$C(x, y) = \begin{cases} 1, & \text{if passes all stages} \\ 0, & \text{otherwise} \end{cases}$$

5.3 Facial Expression Detection

Utilizing convolutional layers, batch normalisation, activation functions, as well as max pooling layers are all part of the facial expression recognition process. Initial pre-processing, reshaping, and normalisation are performed on the supplied facial expression photographs. The convolutional layers take significant details out of the photos and identify patterns associated with various expressions. By normalising the outputs, batch normalisation guarantees stable learning. The activation functions adds non-linearity the in the model capacity to identify advantageous characteristics. The feature maps are downscaled using max pooling layers, concentrating on the most important data. Together, these layers give the deep learning model the ability to reliably identify emotions based on extracted characteristics and recognise and detect facial expressions (Fig. 5).

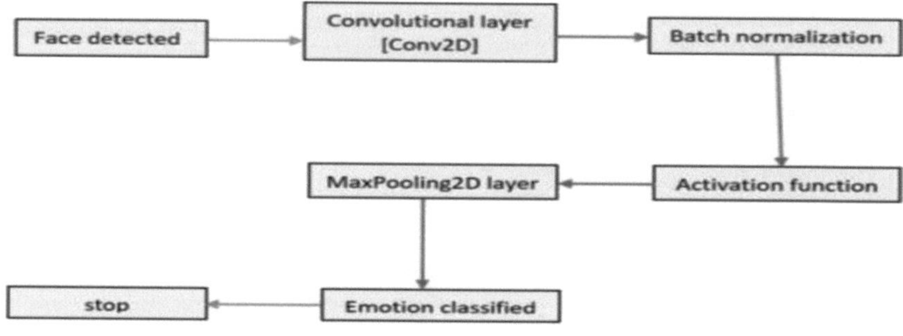

Fig. 5. Flow diagram of layers

5.4 Music Recommendations

The system starts by doing emotional mapping, in which it links particular feelings to associated tunes. Through this mapping, the algorithm is able to locate a number of songs that fit the specified emotion in a database. The playlist is then customised by the system using customization techniques to reflect the user's tastes. It considers elements like the user's musical interests, listening history, and reviews. The technology fine-tunes the playlist to deliver a personalised and pleasurable musical experience by taking into account the user's chosen artists, genres, plus previous interactions.

The system uses a user interface, which could be a web application to present the recommendations for the user after creating the personalised playlist. The interface allows the user to listen to the suggested songs immediately. The system also invites user comment, enabling users to express their thoughts on the suggested songs, enhancing the music recommendations for additional interactions.

6 Results

Proposed techniques, accurately identify user emotions (happiness, sadness, anger, and neutrality). And the system recommended/ played music according to the user's specific mood based on the emotional state detected. This process saved users much time scrolling through extremely large music libraries which was a universal problem music listeners had. The overall results were intuitive, with the users engaging with the system and the 87% accuracy. Model is used to trained on the dataset feb2013 and below shown are the output screen of player after recognizing the emotion (Figs. 6, 7 and 8).

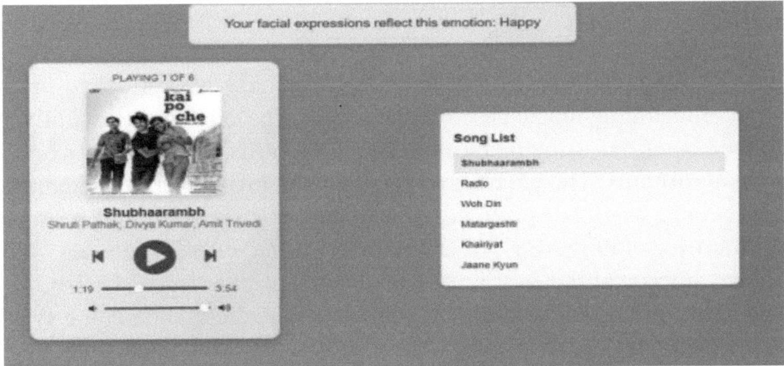

Fig. 6. Screenshot for Happy mood detected

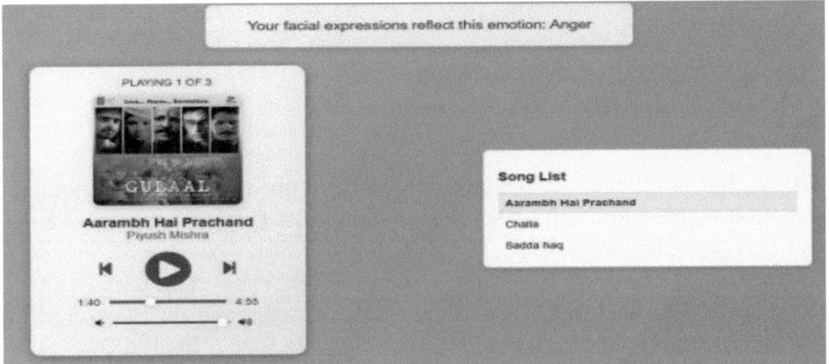

Fig. 7. Screenshot for Anger mood detected

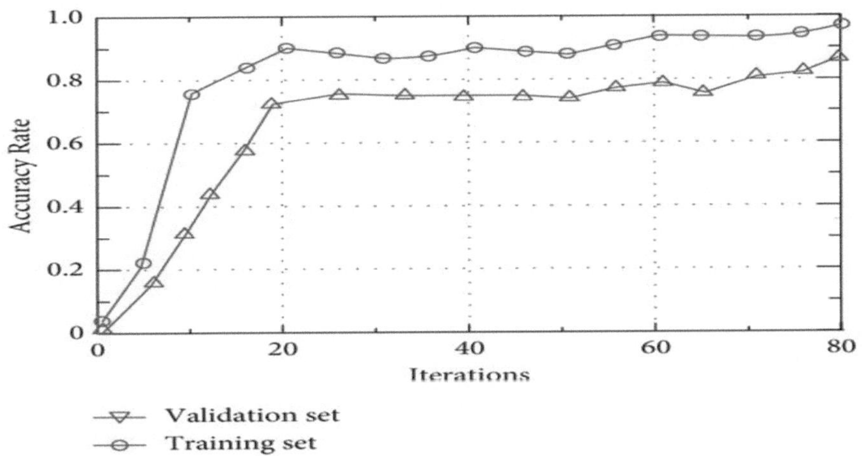

Fig. 8. Accuracy graph

7 Conclusion

Through the use of facial expression analysis, this study was effective in creating a system for recommending music based on emotions. The system successfully identified and categorised emotions using facial expressions by utilising neural networks and face identification algorithms. The creation of personalised music recommendations catered to the user's feelings was made possible by the merging of deep learning techniques with face recognition technology. By offering pertinent and interesting song suggestions, the experiment improved the user's musical listening experience. It also showed the possibilities of integrating emotion detection with music recommendation systems. The results demonstrate how the analysis of facial expressions and machine learning maybe used to build sophisticated and individualized music recommendation systems.

Declaration. The authors declare that they have not used any type of generative artificial intelligence for the writing of this manuscript, nor for the creation of images, graphics, tables, or their corresponding.

References

1. Aljanaki, A., Egede-Nissen, V.: Towards personalized music recommendation system using facial emotion recognition. In: 2019 IEEE International Conference on Systems, Man and Cybernetics (SMC), pp. 4123–4128. IEEE (2019)
2. Liu, C., Chen, X., Gou, L.: A novel music recommendation system based on facial expression recognition. In: 2021 IEEE 4th International Conference on Electronic Information Technology and Computer Engineering (EITCE), pp. 253–257. IEEE (2021)
3. Dhavalikar, A.S., Kulkarni, R.K.: Face recognition and facial expression detection system. In: 2014 International Conference on Communication and Electronics System (ICECS-2014) (2014)
4. Florence, S.M., Uma, M.: Emotional detection and music recommendation system based on user facial expression. IOP Conf. Ser. Mater. Sci. Eng. **912**(6), 062007 (2020). https://doi.org/10.1088/1757-899X/912/6/062007
5. Wang, T.-H., Lien, J.-J.J.: Facial expression recognition system based on rigid and non-rigid motion separation and 3D PoseEstimation. J. Pattern Recognit. **42**(5), 962–977 (2009)
6. Dureha, A.: An accurate algorithm for generating a music playlist based on facial expressions. Int. J. Comput. Appl. **100**(9), 22–27 (2014)
7. Immanuel James, H., James Anto Arnold, J., Maria MasillaRuban, J., Tamilarasan, M., Saranya, R.: Emotion based music recommendation system. IRJET (2019)
8. Chou, S., Chen, C.: A novel music recommendation system based on facial expression recognition and physiological signals. In: Proceedings of the 2020 4th International Conference on Cloud and Big Data Computing, pp. 159–164 (2020)
9. Hsieh, Y.C., Hsu, C.W.: Affective music recommendation system using facial expression recognition and sentiment analysis. In: Proceedings of the 6th International Conference on Control, Automation and Robotics (ICCAR 2021), pp. 383–387 (2021)
10. Chen, L., Lin, C., Yang, S.: Music recommendation system using facial emotion recognition and neural networks. In: Proceedings of the 4th International Conference on Automation, Control and Robotics Engineering (CACRE 2019), pp. 141–144 (2019)
11. More, A.P., Gholap, S.P., Gayke, A.A., Hon, U.D., Rokade, S.M.: Music recommendation system using facial emotion gestures. Int. J. Res. Appl. Sci. Eng. Technol. (2024). https://doi.org/10.22214/ijraset.2024.65090

12. Mahadik, A., Milgir, S., Jagan, V.B., Kavathekar, V., Patel, J.: Mood based music recommendation system. Int. J. Eng. Res. Technol. (IJERT) (2021)
13. Preema, J.S., Rajashree, S.M., Savitri, H.: Review on facial expression-based music player. Int. J. Eng. Res. Technol. (IJERT) **6**(15) (2018). ISSN2278-0181

Emotion Classification of EEG Signals Using Empirical Wavelet Transform

Mukesh Kumar Jadon[1], Bharavi Mishra[1], and Pramod Gaur[2(⊠)]

[1] Department of CSE, The LNM Institute of Information Technology, Jaipur, India
`{mjadon,bharavi.mishra}@lnmiit.ac.in`
[2] Computer Science, Nottingham Trent University, Nottingham, UK
`pramod.gaur@ntu.ac.uk`

Abstract. In contrast to traditional emotion classification using text, speech, and video data, a relatively new approach of using Electroencephalography (EEG) and brain wave patterns is discussed in this paper. EEG is already being used in the medical field to study and diagnose patients with sleep disorders, coma, encephalopathies, epilepsy, and brain tumors. The proposed approach is applied to the prerecorded EEG dataset (DEAP) to classify emotions. Emotions are categorized as Low (class 0) and High (class 1) for four parameters. In this paper, a new approach is carried out to extract the features from the EEG signals using empirical wavelet transform and various entropy computations to remove the dataset's bias towards the majority class. A fusion of the most suitable classification techniques is evaluated by calculating the F1 score as a performance metric. The achieved F1 score is 78.925 for Valence, 70.04 for Arousal, 74.129 for Dominance, and 81.14 for Liking.

Keywords: Emotion Classification · Electroencephalography (EEG) · Empirical Wavelet Transform (EWT) · Signal Entropy

1   Introduction

Sentiment analysis studies of product reviews, social media comments, and chat data have been around for more than three decades [20]. Emotion classification as a subset of sentiment analysis has been a topic of research for a long time. Emotions are the biological states associated with the human body's nervous system, which define our feelings, thought processes, and responses to the surroundings in one or more ways. Traditionally, chats, comments, posts (text), videos, music preference patterns, speech, and facial expressions are used to classify the emotions of a subject. However, recently, studies of brain wave patterns have proved to be a significant and more efficient way to do so. These patterns give more accurate and detailed information about the emotions of the subject, sometimes the subject himself/herself is unaware of. [26].

The recording and study of brain wave patterns is a relatively new concept used for emotion classification, and Electroencephalography (EEG) is used for

A. K. Somani et al. (Eds.): ICNCS 2025, CCIS 2718, pp. 24–36, 2026.
https://doi.org/10.1007/978-3-032-12544-6_3

this purpose. EEG is a typically noninvasive, electrophysiological monitoring method to record the electrical activities of the brain via electrodes placed on the scalp surface. They tend to have a low signal-to-noise (SNR) ratio [7,10,11,25].

The major step to handle this problem would be to obtain high-SNR EEG signals. There are research groups that have studied the decomposition of single-channel and multi-channel EEG signals to enhance the SNR ratio [8,9]. The brain cells communicate with each other through electrical impulses. EEG measures the electric field generated when thousands of neurons fire in sync and create this electric impulse. These impulses are strong enough to be measured on the head scalp surface. EEG electrode CAPs are used to carry out the electrode placement, making it easier to affix the electrodes to the scalp precisely having sufficient contact with each other. With the help of it, even the activity within cortical areas at sub-second timescales can be detected.

EEG based emotion classification is more robust to stimuli changes and psychological factors that result in repression of feelings that leads to oblivious emotions. This method could prove beneficial for medical applications, product development for disabled people like music recommendation systems, smart systems, etc. and brain computer interface applications [23].

In this research work, the pre-recorded and pre-processed EEG signals from the DEAP dataset [14] has been used and the emotions have been classified as Low and High for four labels, named Valence, Arousal, Dominance and Liking. In psychological terms, Valence indicates the intrinsic pleasure or hatred/aversiveness associated with a stimulus, object, or situation. A high valence level maps to positive feelings such as happy, surprised, protected, joyous, satisfied, etc., whereas a low valence maps to the emotions related to being sad, frightened, or angry. Arousal is the quantitative degree of physiological and psychological activation level. On a scale of 0–9, 0 indicates the subject being least excited and 9 indicates the most excited state. Most of the previous works on DEAP dataset use just these two labels, i.e. Valence and Arousal to form two-dimensional models for emotion classification [24]. Further, Dominance indicates the control factor. A high dominance value indicates the emotion of dominating or controlling over the situation, for example, when a person is aggressive, while a low value indicates being dominated by or controlled by the situation, for example, when the person is frightened by the stimulus. Lastly, Liking is the scale of simply liking (high value) or disliking (low value) of a stimulus. Analyzing all four aspects of emotions gives detailed information about the emotions of the subject based on the changes in the stimuli. In the case of DEAP dataset, as discussed in the coming sections, the stimuli are 60-second videos(the EEG patterns) of the subjects were recorded while showing several one-minute videos to the subjects.

In this paper, a fusion of classification approaches like Support Vector Machine (SVM), K-Nearest Neighbour (KNN), and Random Forest is applied and analysed to classify these four labels as 0 (Low) and 1 (High). Techniques such as Empirical Wavelet Transform (EWT), entropy-based feature extraction, changing threshold, and oversampling of the minority class have been proposed to reduce bias. The rest of the paper is organised as follows: Section 2 brief overview of the previous research works in the stated field. Section 3 describes the DEAP dataset. Section 4 presents the proposed research methodology, including data pre-processing and model selection. Section 5 compares the proposed results with those of the previous works. Finally, the conclusions are presented in section 6 followed by references.

2   Related Work

A lot of previous research has been successfully done in the field of emotion classification [1,4,17–19,27,29,31,32]. And the data used for these works range widely from text, videos, facial expressions, speech signals, to the browser search and other online behavioral patterns [2,15,30].

One of the widely used previous works is the bipolar model, where only the Arousal and Valence labels are considered for classification because degree of pleasure/displeasure and arousal accounted for almost all the variances for other commonly used scales of measuring effect (scales of happiness, elation, anger, fear, anxiety, and depression) of emotions. This emotion classification approach is advocated by Russell [24]. Whereas Plutchik defines eight basic emotion states: anger, fear, sadness, disgust, surprise, anticipation, acceptance, and joy, all other emotions are derivable from these basic emotions [22].

Many researchers have used other machine learning techniques to analyze and classify EEG data. According to one of the surveys conducted for this purpose by Rani[20], KNN and SVM are two of the most widely used techniques for classifying EEG data. This claim is supported by the works of others as well [13, 21,28,33]. Other widely proposed researches are based on Deep Neural Network, Bayesian Network, and Regression tree. [3,6].

The comparison of these results solely based on accuracy would not be sufficient and justified, the results can be misled towards the majority class if the dataset is not balanced. Different evaluation metrics, feature selection methods, and classification models account for different results and are chosen according to the requirements and application of the research. In this paper, the F1 score is used as an evaluation metric, and the fusion of classification models such as SVM, KNN, Random Forest, feature extraction based on varying entropies, and finding the optimal threshold value have been analyzed.

3   Dataset

In this paper, the DEAP dataset [14] is used. Since the release of this dataset, a lot of research has been conducted on emotion classification using EEG and proving the ease of availability and reliability of the dataset. The DEAP presents a multimodal dataset for the analysis of human affective states and contains the recording of the EEG signals of 32 participants. Each one of them watched 40 videos of one-minute-long. Then the participants rated each video in terms of the levels of Valence, Arousal, Dominance, and Liking on a scale of 0–9.

The original unprocessed data file contains 32 .bdf files (Bio Semi's data format), each with 48 recorded channels at 512 Hz for 40 trials. We have used the pre-processed data files which were available in .dat format (pickled python/numpy), well suited for applying classification and regression techniques. Pre-processing involved down sampling to 128 Hz, removal of EEG artifacts, and passing through a bandpass filter of 4–45 Hz. For each trial the video is of 63 s (including 3 s pretrial), so we have 8064 samples for each trial(Table 1).

Table 1. Structure of .DAT FILE for SUBJECT-1 (same for all 32 SUBJECTS)

Key	Value (type=array)	Array shape
Data	Trial x channel x samples	40 × 40 x 8064
Labels	Trial x label rating	40 × 4
	(valence, arousal, dominance, liking)	

The final dataset contains 32 .dat files, one for each subject, containing a hash data structure with keys, namely 'data' and 'labels', and their values in the form of arrays. The key 'data' has 8064 numerical values of samples recorded for 40 trials (videos)from each of the 40 channel/electrode, whereas the 'labels' key has values of the 40 trials for the four labels, namely Valence, Arousal, Dominance, and Liking.

Table 2. Structure of .DAT FILE after taking 32 CHANNELS

Key	Value (type=array)	Array shape
Data	Trial x channel x samples	40 × 32 x 8064
Labels	Trial x label rating	40 × 4
	(valence, arousal, dominance, liking)	

4   Methodology

A rigorous exercise is done between data collection and finally making predictions using machine learning models. Data cleaning, data preprocessing, choosing a suitable model for the task then training and evaluating the model, tuning hyperparameters are some of the basic steps included. The choice of data preprocessing steps, feature selection procedure, and classification models all play a major role in determining better results for emotion classification using EEG compared to the previous works. Figure 1 depicts the detailed explanation of the methods chosen for this paper.

4.1   Data Preprocessing

The preprocessed files, each for 32 subjects of DEAP dataset consisted of data for 8064 samples from 40 channels each for 40 different videos. Out of those 40 channels, 8 were peripheral channels, so data was taken from the leftover 32 channels for analyzing the emotions. The final structure of the dataset is detailed in the Table 2.

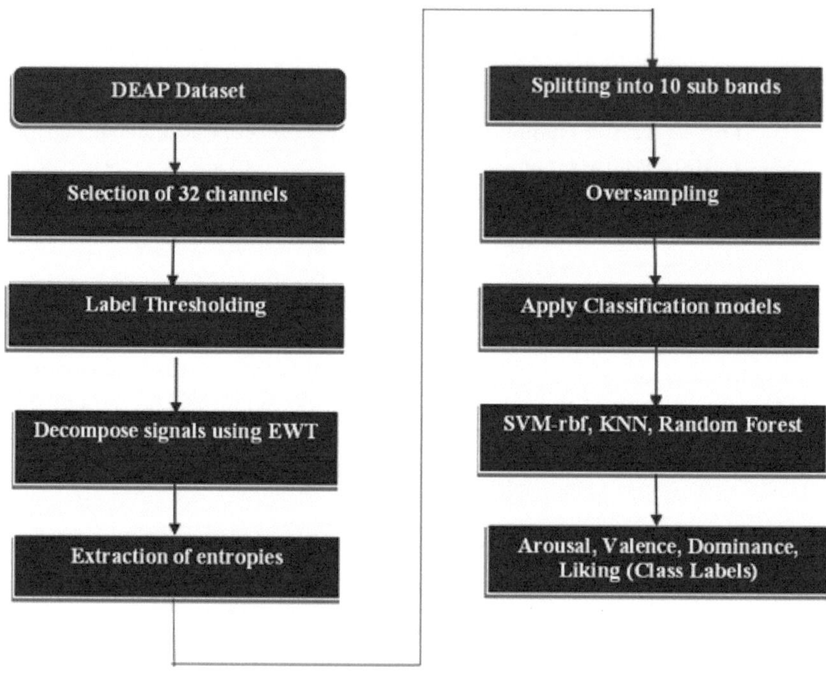

Fig. 1. Flow-chart of the proposed methodology.

Changing Threshold Values: The emotion labels- Valence, Arousal, Dominance and Liking, are each represented with a score on a scale of 0–9, where 0 denote lowest and 9 highest value for the label. To classify these labels as Low (0) and High (1), the scores were converted to binary encoding using a threshold: scores above the threshold were encoded as '1'(High), while those below were encoded as '0'(Low). In most of the previous studies, the threshold value was strictly set to 4.5, which is the mean of the 09 scale. In the proposed method, the results of the optimal model are recorded with varying threshold values ranging from 3.5 to 7 and the best results were observed at the threshold of 3.5, followed by 5.5 and 7 (can be verified from Fig. 2). In other cases, when not specified, the threshold value was set to 3.5 to optimize the results. The best results were achieved by considering every 32nd feature, resulting in a total of 8064 features extracted for each 1280 videos.

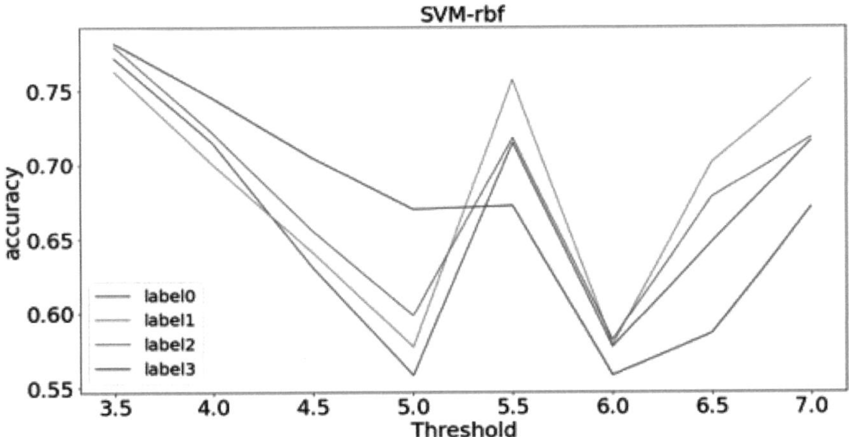

Fig. 2. Accuracy score of SVM (rbf kernel) model with varying threshold values.

Feature Extraction: The DEAP is a time series dataset consisting of amplitude values recorded at different time intervals; these amplitude values can not be directly used as features. Thus, an emerging signal processing technique, "Empirical Wavelet Transform(EWT)" was applied to extract the signal entropies as the features to train the model. The process starts with the decomposition of the recorded signals using EWT, and then various entropies were calculated, such as Permutation entropies (PE), Spectral entropies (SE), Singular value decomposition entropies (SvdEn), Approximate entropies (ApEn) and Sample entropies (SampEn).

Empirical Wavelet Transform: The empirical wavelet transform is a technique that creates segments of the signal spectrum using an adaptive wavelet subdivision scheme. In this paper this technique is used to create 10 sub-bands based on frequency, which helped in further analysis. Different models are applied to analyze each band, and the reported results are found to be different for these models.

EWT Decomposition: The input signal x(t) is decomposed into different empirical wavelet sub-bands:

$$x(t) = C_0(t) + \sum_{n=1}^{N} d_n \psi_n(t) \tag{1}$$

Where C_0 and d_n are the empirical wavelet coefficients obtained via: $C_0 = \langle x, \psi \rangle, \quad d_n = (x, \psi, \psi_n)$

Reconstruction Formula: The original signal is reconstructed using the inverse EWT:

$$x(t) = \sum_{n=0}^{N} \langle x, \psi \rangle \psi_n(t) \tag{2}$$

4.2 Entropies

The entropy of a signal describes the distribution of signal components [16]. Extracting entropies for a signal is a nonlinear method and is suitable to study EEG signals. After dividing the signals into ten subsequent sub bands, different entropies were calculated for each sub band. Following are the entropies which are used in the proposed model:

Permutation Entropy (PE): It is a robust time series tool which provides a quantification measure of the complexity of a dynamic system by capturing the order relations between values of a time series and extracting a probability distribution of the ordinal patterns.

Spectral Entropy (SE): It is a measure of signal irregularity, which sums the normalized signal spectral power.

Singular Value Decomposition Entropy (SvdEn): It characterizes information content or regularity of a signal depending on the number of vectors attributed to the process.

Approximate Entropy (ApEn): It is a technique used to quantify the amount of regularity and the unpredictability of fluctuation over time-series data.

Sample Entropy (SampEn): It is a modification of approximate entropies used for accessing the complexity of physiological time series signals, diagnosing disease states.

4.3 Oversampling

Oversampling is the process of duplicating data samples from a minority class, and it is done to adjust the class of distribution of a dataset and reduce biases without loss of actual data. The DEAP dataset is highly biased with most of the data samples accounting to positive values of labels (Valence, Arousal, Dominance and Liking). So training and testing on such dataset, the traditional models result in large number of False Positives (FP). This is a classic case when a model predicts True value without considering the features, although this could result in high accuracy, but model is not reliable. Oversampling of minority class was carried out in the proposed approach to make the model robust and reliable with a better F1 score,

4.4   Models

After preprocessing the data, extracting entropies, and applying oversampling, in the proposed method, the classification algorithms like support vector machine (SVM) with RBF kernel, K-nearest neighbors (KNN), Naive Bayes, Logistic Regression, and Random Forest were applied to train the model. As mentioned earlier, the rating of each video was done for all four labels on a scale of 0–9. To classify it as High (label 1) or Low (label 0), a threshold value was set from 3.5 to 7 in the interval of 0.5 that fetched more accurate results for future predictions. The received results are plotted in Fig. 3, and it is evident that most models give their best results for the threshold of 3.5.

SVM classifier plots the data points in n-dimensional space and finds a hyperplane to differentiate between the two classes with maximum margin. Support vectors are the data points that are closest to the hyperplane and help in maximizing the distance between the data points of different classes so as to make future predictions with more accuracy. This algorithm also ignore the outliers. It performs well when there are large number of features compared to the number of examples which are in our case.

SVM uses kernels that take low dimensional input data space and convert it to high dimensional space to convert non-separable data into separable. All the kernels of SVM use a different equation to determine the hyperplane. RBF kernel function returns the value of the inner product of two points which define similarity in high dimension space. SVM with radial basis function (rbf) kernel outperforms other models and results in the highest accuracy of 77.1% and KNN performs the same. Other SVM kernels also followed with the nearly same score of 76.9% and 75.9%.

$$K(X1, X2) = exp(-\gamma \|X1 - X2\|^2) \tag{3}$$

where $\|X1 - X2\|$ is the Euclidean distance between $X1$ and $X2$
,

In contrast, the KNN algorithm, which also performs with the same accuracy as SVM, is a supervised machine learning algorithm that works on the principle of feature similarity. It computes the Euclidean, Hamming or Manhattan distance between the new data points with every training example. The model picks K entries which are closest to the data point. Then with the help of majority voting, the most common label is considered as a class for the new data point. In the proposed work, we took value of K as 13 to pick 13 topmost similar data points and predict with the most common label.

Another algorithm used in this work is Random Forest. The term forest represents that it is an ensemble of decision trees. In this, data is trained using

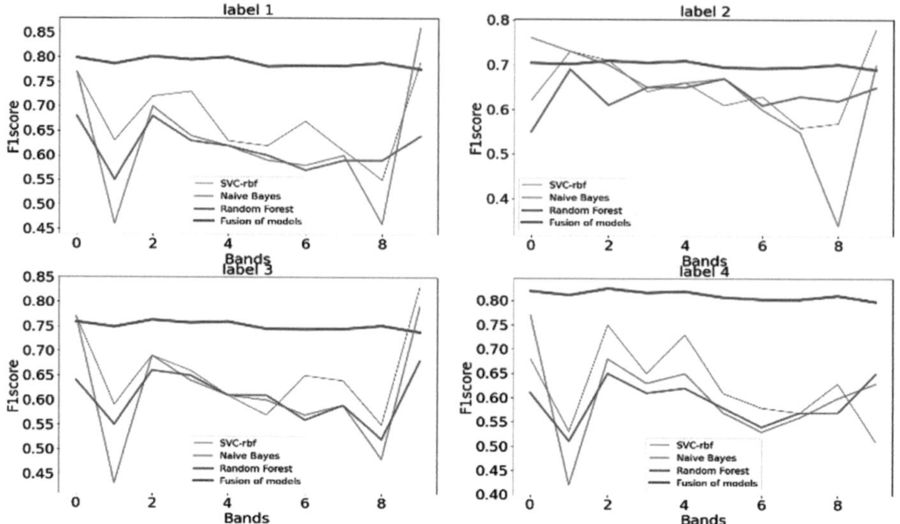

Fig. 3. F1 score vs Band for four labels applying different models.

the bagging method in which combination of learning models increases the overall result. Each individual decision tree gives a class prediction and the class with the majority becomes the model's prediction. Trees are taken to be relatively uncorrelated so that they protect each other from their individual errors. While splitting a node in the tree it looks for best feature among a random subset of features and it is easy to measure the relative importance of each feature on prediction. The overfitting can be minimised by dropping some of the features not required.

Naive Bayes is the classifier that works based on Bayes theorem. It takes continuous values associated with each feature that is assumed to be distributed according to a Gaussian distribution. Bayes theorem is defined as:

$$P\left(\frac{A}{B}\right) = \frac{P\left(\frac{B}{A}\right) * (P(A)}{P(B)} \tag{4}$$

Here, Naive assumption is that A and B are independent sets which imply: $P(A, B) = P(A) * P(B)$

$$So \ y = argmax_y(P(y)\prod_{i=1}^{n} P(x_i|y)) \tag{5}$$

where $P(y)$ is class probability and $P(x_i/y)$ is called conditional probability.

5   Results and Discussion

The result of our fusion of models with unbiased oversampled data is shown below in Table 3 for each sub band and their corresponding label. Label 4 consistently exhibited the highest values (ranging from 79.87 to 82.51), and Label 2 displayed the lowest (69.01 to 70.93). Among the bands, Band 3 demonstrated superior performance, achieving peak scores for Label 1 (80.11), Label 3 (76.29), and Label 4 (82.51), whereas Band 10 yielded the lowest results across all labels. The experimental results show that Label 4 typically demonstrates the highest values (ranging from 79.87 to 82.51), and Label 2 exhibits the lowest (69.01 to 70.93). Another interesting observation is that Band 3 achieved peak scores for Label 1 (80.11), Label 3 (76.29), and Label 4 (82.51), whereas Band 10 yielded the lowest for all labels. Each label indicates minor variation, though the magnitude of difference needs further statistical evaluation. Label 4 and Band 3 potentially offer enhanced discriminative capabilities, and these findings lead to feature selection or model refinement. Future research should focus on statistical verification and investigating the factors contributing to these performance differences.

Table 3. Results for 10 bands and four labels

Band/Label	Label 1	Label 2	Label 3	Label 4
Band 1	79.811	70.407	75.895	81.932
Band 2	78.617	70.156	74.859	81.122
Band 3	80.113	70.931	76.287	82.505
Band 4	79.481	70.516	75.732	81.646
Band 5	80.002	70.909	75.975	81.897
Band 6	78.120	69.479	74.514	80.729
Band 7	78.319	69.317	74.443	80.320
Band 8	78.274	69.527	74.513	80.331
Band 9	78.896	70.156	75.184	81.089
Band 10	77.616	69.009	73.888	79.870

In Table 4, the proposed results are compared with different previous works for the experiment of emotion classification using EEG data. Table 4 demonstrate a significant improvement in emotion recognition performance using our proposed approach compared to previous studies. Our model achieves an F1 score of 78. 90% for valence and 70.04% for arousal, outperforming the strongest prior work (Chen et al. [5]) by 9.94% and 2.21%, respectively. These results indicate that our method effectively enhances feature representation and classification accuracy for emotional states. Compared to Koelstra et al. [14], our model improves valence recognition by 15.8% and arousal recognition by 7.4%, underscoring the robustness of our approach. The lowest-performing model (Daniela

Girardi [12]) highlights the challenge of arousal detection, where our method still achieves a 13.74% improvement. To validate these findings, a statistical significance analysis was conducted, ensuring that the observed gains are not due to random variations. However, the relatively smaller increase in arousal recognition suggests ongoing challenges in capturing subtle activation intensity variations, necessitating future research into temporal modeling, self-supervised learning, and domain adaptation techniques to further improve performance.

Table 4. Results Comparison With other research work and the proposed work.

Author	F1 Score Valance	F1 Score Arousal
Koelstra [14]	63.10	65.20
Jin Chen [5]	68.96	67.83
Deniala Girardi [12]	63.10	65.20
Proposed	**78.90**	**70.04**

6   Conclusion

In this research work, we presented observations on the classification of emotions with EEG brain waves using the DEAP dataset. The aim was to improve the F1 score of previous research done on the same. Although the accuracy is almost the same, the F1 score was improved, and thus, this work can reduce False Positives, resulting in a more robust model. In this paper, we discuss, starting with a selection of threshold values for labels, to the extraction of features after applying EWT, and finally, oversampling the data set to feed into the classification models. The best classification model for this classification can be the fusion of models SVM, KNN, and, Random Forest. To compare the results, we used references from previous works. These analyses will help us in our future work by applying different techniques to get a working application. In the future, it will be interesting to try other multi-channel decomposition techniques like multivariate variational decomposition and multivariate empirical mode decomposition with the latest deep learning models, including CNN and Graph neural networks.

Declaration

The proposed paper has been written exclusively by the authors mentioned in the paper. Online resources such as AI tools or digital reference materials are not used for drawing tables, figures, etc. All of the content in the article is based on our own understanding, analysis, and original thought process.

References

1. Alarcao, S.M., Fonseca, M.J.: Emotions recognition using EEG signals: a survey. IEEE Trans. Affect. Comput. **10**(3), 374–393 (2017)
2. Bhaskar, J., Sruthi, K., Nedungadi, P.: Hybrid approach for emotion classification of audio conversation based on text and speech mining. Procedia Comput. Sci. **46**, 635–643 (2015)
3. Brown, L.E., Tsamardinos, I., Aliferis, C.F.: A novel algorithm for scalable and accurate Bayesian network learning. In: Medinfo, pp. 711–715 (2004)
4. Chen, G., Hou, R.: A new machine double-layer learning method and its application in non-linear time series forecasting. In: 2007 International Conference on Mechatronics and Automation, pp. 795–799. IEEE (2007)
5. Chen, J., Hu, B., Moore, P., Zhang, X., Ma, X.: Electroencephalogram-based emotion assessment system using ontology and data mining techniques. Appl. Soft Comput. **30**, 663–674 (2015)
6. Downey, S., Russell, M.: A decision tree approach to task-independent speech recognition. Proc. Instit. Acoustics **14**, p181–p181 (1992)
7. Gaur, P., Gupta, H., Chowdhury, A., McCreadie, K., Pachori, R.B., Wang, H.: A sliding window common spatial pattern for enhancing motor imagery classification in EEG-BCI. IEEE Trans. Instrum. Meas. **70**, 1–9 (2021)
8. Gaur, P., McCreadie, K., Pachori, R.B., Wang, H., Prasad, G.: An automatic subject specific channel selection method for enhancing motor imagery classification in EEG-BCI using correlation. Biomed. Signal Process. Control **68**, 102574 (2021)
9. Gaur, P., Pachori, R.B., Wang, H., Prasad, G.: An empirical mode decomposition based filtering method for classification of motor-imagery EEG signals for enhancing brain-computer interface. In: 2015 International joint conference on neural networks (IJCNN), pp. 1–7. IEEE (2015)
10. Gaur, P., Pachori, R.B., Wang, H., Prasad, G.: A multi-class EEG-based BCI classification using multivariate empirical mode decomposition based filtering and Riemannian geometry. Expert Syst. Appl. **95**, 201–211 (2018)
11. Gaur, P., Pachori, R.B., Wang, H., Prasad, G.: An automatic subject specific intrinsic mode function selection for enhancing two-class EEG-based motor imagery-brain computer interface. IEEE Sens. J. **19**(16), 6938–6947 (2019)
12. Girardi, D., Lanubile, F., Novielli, N.: Emotion detection using noninvasive low cost sensors. In: 2017 seventh international conference on affective computing and intelligent interaction (ACII), pp. 125–130. IEEE (2017)
13. Huang, W.Y., Shen, X.Q., Wu, Q.: Classify the number of EEG current sources using support vector machines. In: Proceedings International Conference on Machine Learning and Cybernetics. vol. 4, pp. 1793–1795. IEEE (2002)
14. Koelstra, S., et al.: Deap: a database for emotion analysis; using physiological signals. IEEE Trans. Affect. Comput. **3**(1), 18–31 (2011)
15. Li, W., Xu, H.: Text-based emotion classification using emotion cause extraction. Expert Syst. Appl. **41**(4), 1742–1749 (2014)
16. Liang, Z., et al.: EEG entropy measures in anesthesia. Front. Comput. Neurosci. **9**, 16 (2015)
17. Liu, Y., Sourina, O.: EEG-based valence level recognition for real-time applications. In: 2012 international conference on cyberworlds, pp. 53–60. IEEE (2012)
18. Liu, Y., Sourina, O.: EEG databases for emotion recognition. In: 2013 international conference on cyberworlds, pp. 302–309. IEEE (2013)

19. Liu, Y., Sourina, O., Nguyen, M.K.: Real-time EEG-based human emotion recognition and visualization. In: 2010 international conference on cyberworlds, pp. 262–269. IEEE (2010)

20. Mäntylä, M.V., Graziotin, D., Kuutila, M.: The evolution of sentiment analysis-a review of research topics, venues, and top cited papers. Comput. Sci. Rev. **27**, 16–32 (2018)

21. Parvin, H., Alizadeh, H., Minaei-Bidgoli, B.: MKNN: modified k-nearest neighbor. In: Proceedings of the world congress on engineering and computer science. vol. 1. Newswood Limited (2008)

22. Plutchik, R.: Emotions and life: perspectives from psychology, biology, and evolution. American Psychological Association (2003)

23. Ramzan, M., Dawn, S.: A survey of brainwaves using electroencephalography (EEG) to develop robust brain-computer interfaces (BCIs): processing techniques and algorithms. In: 2019 9th International Conference on Cloud Computing, Data Science and Engineering (Confluence), pp. 642–647. IEEE (2019)

24. Russell, J.A.: Affective space is bipolar. J. Pers. Soc. Psychol. **37**(3), 345 (1979)

25. Saideepthi, P., Chowdhury, A., Gaur, P., Pachori, R.B.: Sliding window along with EEGNet-based prediction of EEG motor imagery. IEEE Sens. J. **23**(15), 17703–17713 (2023)

26. Shaari, N., Syafiq, M., Amin, M., Mikami, O.: Electroencephalography (EEG) application in neuromarketing-exploring the subconscious mind. J. Adv. Manuf. Tech. (JAMT) 13(2 (2)) (2019)

27. Sohaib, A.T., Qureshi, S., Hagelbäck, J., Hilborn, O., Jerčić, P.: Evaluating classifiers for emotion recognition using EEG. In: Foundations of Augmented Cognition: 7th International Conference, AC 2013, Held as Part of HCI International 2013, Las Vegas, NV, USA, July 21-26, 2013. Proceedings 7, pp. 492–501. Springer (2013)

28. Tangermann, M., Winkler, I., Haufe, S., Blankertz, B.: Classification of artifactual ICA components. Int J Bioelectromagnetism **11**(2), 110–114 (2009)

29. Tripathi, S., Acharya, S., Sharma, R., Mittal, S., Bhattacharya, S.: Using deep and convolutional neural networks for accurate emotion classification on DEAP data. In: Proceedings of the AAAI Conference on Artificial Intelligence. vol. 31, pp. 4746–4752 (2017)

30. Verma, G.K., Tiwary, U.S.: Multimodal fusion framework: a multiresolution approach for emotion classification and recognition from physiological signals. Neuroimage **102**, 162–172 (2014)

31. Wang, Q., Sourina, O., Nguyen, M.K.: Fractal dimension based neurofeedback in serious games. Vis. Comput. **27**, 299–309 (2011)

32. Xu, H., Plataniotis, K.N.: Affective states classification using EEG and semi-supervised deep learning approaches. In: 2016 IEEE 18th International Workshop on Multimedia Signal Processing (MMSP), pp. 1–6. IEEE (2016)

33. Yu, Y.H., Lai, P.C., Ko, L.W., Chuang, C.H., Kuo, B.C., Lin, C.T.: An EEG-based classification system of Passenger's motion sickness level by using feature extraction/selection technologies. In: The 2010 international joint conference on neural networks (IJCNN), pp. 1–6. IEEE (2010)

Next-Gen Networking
and Communication Systems

A Unified Platform for Influencer-Brand Collaboration via YouTube Analytics

Shaila Pawar, Ananya Shetty$^{(\boxtimes)}$, Siddhi Suryavanshi, and Sujal Poojari

Information Technology, A.C. Patil College of Engineering, Kharghar, Maharashtra, India
`{skdeore,ananyacshetty}@acpce.ac.in`

Abstract. The rise of influencer marketing has significantly transformed advertising methods, Due to its recent developments, influencer marketing stands as a pillar in the advertising ecosystem, with content creators on YouTube central to brand equity. This paper discusses a scalable data-driven platform that narrows the gap between niche YouTube creators and brand personnel. The platform incorporates predictive video performance analytics, intuitive dashboards for different user roles, and automated features to manage collaboration. Using regression techniques, Next.js, Prisma ORM, and the YouTube Data API, the system manages operational efficiency as well as predicting engagement in the future. Its core modules provide low levels of channel performance analytics, smart filtering, and admin oversight. The platform empowers YouTubers and brands to make informed decisions through real-time insights, ultimately enhancing collaboration effectiveness and campaign outcomes.

Keywords: YouTube influencer marketing · predictive analytics · Next.js · Prisma ORM · YouTube Data API · brand collaboration

1 Introduction

Research shows that in the changing world of digital media, YouTube has shifted into a preferred avenue for publishing content to reach audiences and marketing practices. The specificity of such high growth in the number of content creators on YouTube and brands has opened up an even more complex playground, and thus, finding a fit influencer for the right brand becomes an opportunity as well as a challenge. The increase in the number of content creators and brands on YouTube has created a complicated environment, and here lies the challenge of fitting the right influencer with the appropriate brand, which offers both prospects and difficulties. The overriding purpose of this project is to create a complete framework within which all parties, YouTubers, brand representatives, and general users alike, will be able to interact more freely, incorporating foresights, predictions, and collaboration tools too. The framework contains three main parts: public landing page, more specific influencer and brand owner's dashboards, and admin panel managing the entire system. This landing page serves as an access point for users to view different YouTube channels via the YouTube Data API. It accesses channel details

A. K. Somani et al. (Eds.): ICNCS 2025, CCIS 2718, pp. 39–51, 2026.
https://doi.org/10.1007/978-3-032-12544-6_4

including subscriber counts, total views, geographical location, and performance statistics of the last five videos. The system also contains a regression algorithm to predict the viewership of a forthcoming video to offer insights on likely audience reach to enhance user participation. It allows a personalized dashboard for YouTube influencers where they will register their channels, set brand preferences, and allow collaboration requests. Tools provide brand owners to segregate influencers on the basis of subscriber count, geographical area, or video performance and approach for collaboration through detailed proposal documents.

Moreover, this speed-of-light interaction is facilitated with the aid of a notification system ensuring rapid communication between influencers and brands. An admin panel manages all of the operations by providing the functionalities to approve or deny influencer registrations, track collaborations, and conserve the integrity of the system. On the backend, reliable data management, scalability, and reliability are ensured by the use of Prisma ORM. Apart from simplifying the cycle of interaction, the solution also brings the predictive analytics concept to improve the decision-making process of influencers and companies alike. The model solves the inefficiencies of the traditional cooperation model and offers actionable data for the stakeholders. It automates some critical elements of influencer marketing and makes use of real-time analytics. This study quite vividly delves into the architecture and features of the implementation details that provide a fully integrated framework for brand-influencer engagement on YouTube. This trailblazing can really change how brands interact with influencers by exploiting technology to drive efficiency and bringing more data to the center in the influencer marketing ecosystem.

2   Related Work

Increasingly, social media such as YouTube is becoming increasingly popular as a source of influencer marketing. Consequently, a research effort has been invested in its effect on brand engagement, content performance, and user interaction. The many facets of influencer marketing are overlaid on a few works-the analytical and psychological. However, those efforts are silent when it comes to practical, integrated solutions of the scalable and automated type.

Kumar [1] shows the incisive power of UGC for brand perception but lacks actionable frameworks for matchmaking between brands and influencers. Chen et al. [2] studied the parasocial bond between the influencers and the audience in their work and showed its importance regarding the engagement of users but did not look at the analytic tools required for a perfect plan regarding collaboration. Similar studies were conducted by Basile et al. [3] on co-creation in luxury brand communities, whose emphasis was on interactive social change rather than on tech driven scalable influencer-brand integration.

At the same time, targeting the use of data analytics for improved brand-influencer alignment is initiated by Bansal et al. [4] but there is absence of automation and intuitive user interfaces. The current platforms and tools complement these challenges; some have static measures that do not go beyond counting some subscribers: No dynamic engagement forecasting was created, and no governance in place for the management of collaborations. According to Okonkwo and Namkoisse [6], creating and sustaining authentic relationships remains one of the greatest challenges in fragmented systems.

Although Chen et al. [7] focused extensively on dissection of popular video strategies, they did not venture into predictive modeling.

To overcome those limitations, the proposed system establishes dynamic analytics combined with predictive modeling, personalized dashboards, and real-time data drawn from the YouTube Data API. The present work uses regression algorithms to forecast performances of videos while reliant on an admin panel for improvements in automation, governance, novel research, and scalability (Table 1).

Table. 1. Comparative Summary

Prior Work	Focus Area	Identified Limitation	Our System's Contribution
Kumar [1]	UGC and brand perception	No practical matchmaking tools	Provides predictive influencer-brand matching
Chen et al. [2]	Parasocial interactions	Lacks predictive analytics	Incorporates video engagement forecasting
Basile et al. [3]	Value co-creation in fashion UGC	Industry-specific and non-scalable	Scalable platform for multi-domain use
Bansal et al. [4]	Data analytics for influencer selection	No automation or end-user interface	Offers full-stack automation with intuitive UI
Okonkwo & Namkoisse [6]	Brand-influencer relationships	No structured system for trust-building	Ensures transparency via admin panel
Chen et al. [7]	Video structure analysis	No integration with performance prediction models	Uses regression to forecast content performance

3 Methodology

3.1 System Architecture

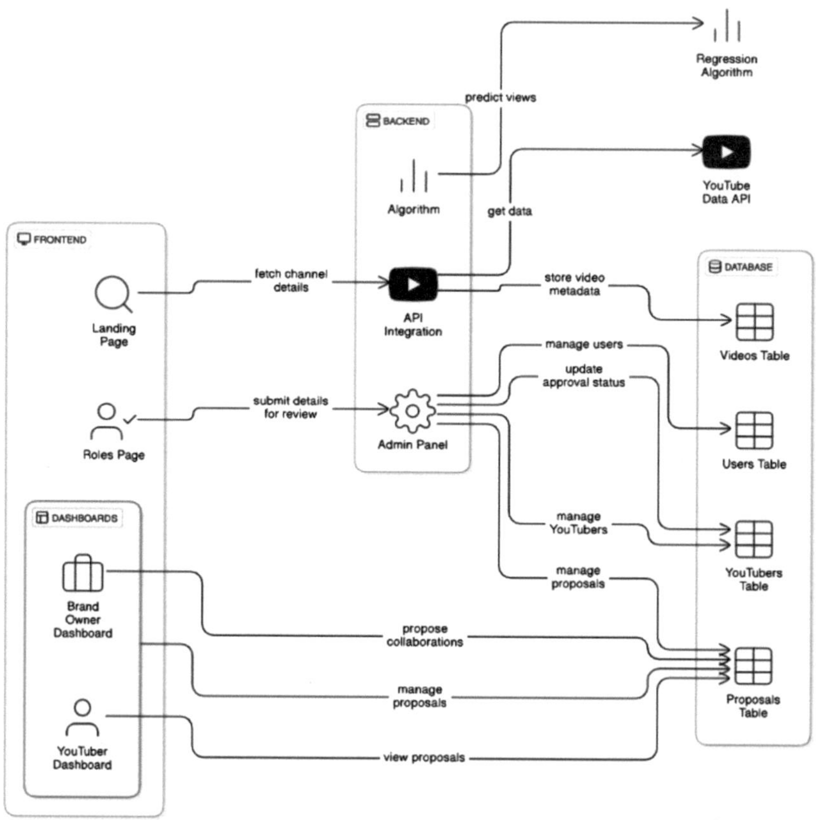

Fig. 1. System Architecture

The system architecture allows for the layered interaction of YouTubers and brand owners, which occurs along a three-layered scheme: the frontend, backend, and database. The frontend developed in Next.js exposes user dashboards—general users can engage with YouTube channels using the YouTube Data API while influencers and brands manage metrics, proposals, and targeted searches. The backend also in Next.js, provides API integration and business logic for predictive analytics through linear regression, with database operations via the Prisma ORM. The integrated admin panel allows for user registration and profile verification and offers admin control over proposals. The data are kept in a PostgreSQL database, organized around entities like users, channels, videos, and campaigns. The architecture prioritizes modularity, responsiveness to real-time changes, and scalability toward an efficient and user-friendly solution (Fig. 1).

3.2 Functional Modules

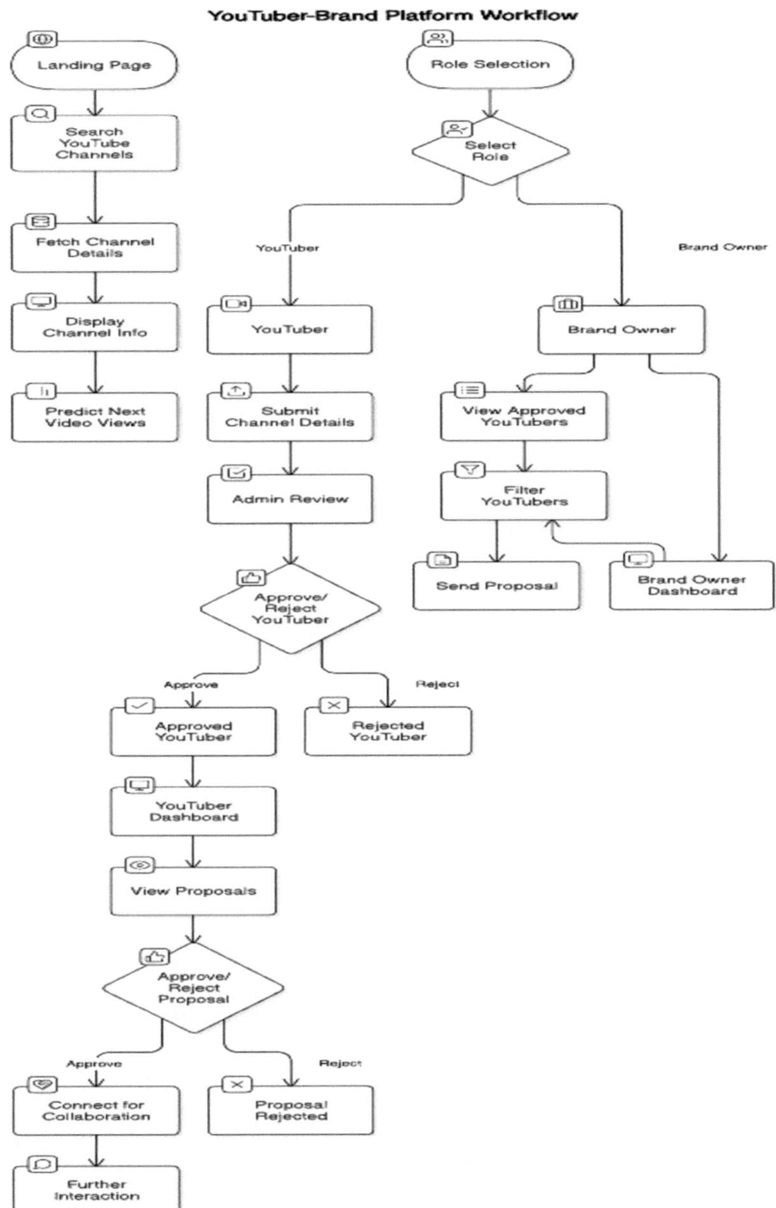

Fig. 2. Workflow of the system

The platform consists of a number of functional modules that work together to improve user experience and the functionality of the system (Fig. 2):

User Role Selection Module

In signing up, users select either influencer or brand role that activates features based on their selection. Influencers manage channels and proposals; brands filter and connect to creators.

YouTuber Channel Management Module

This module allows influencers to securely link their YouTube accounts for performance monitoring and predictive insight. The Influencers may also respond to collaboration proposals.

Brand Owner Search and Filter Module

Brands can use advanced filters to search for and shortlist creators, such as niche, geography, subscriber count, and engagement. Predictive analytics help in identifying high-performing channels.

Collaboration Proposal Management Module

Automates the entire proposal life cycle-from creation, submission, and acceptance, to status tracking-and makes communication transparent between brands and influencers throughout the lifespan of the proposal.

Dashboard Module

This module provides dashboards unique to each role. Influencers can see channel analytics and proposals, brand owners can manage campaigns and interactions, and admins can oversee how the system is being used as well as validating users.

Admin Management Module

The administration of the platform involves profile verification, management of proposals, resolution of conflicts, and analysis and reporting of statistics to monitor usage of the platform.

Analytics and Reporting Module

It provides data-driven insights on video performance, audience engagement, and the impact generated by the campaign. Insights are available in printed format or exportable for use during strategic decision-making.

These functional components harmoniously interact with one another, contributing to the seamless experience for the users. Structure encourages modularity, scalability, and easy maintenance by distributing tasks among well-defined modules. The fusion of advanced analytics, intuitive interface, and strong management capabilities ensures that this platform is performant and influential.

3.3 Data Collection and Processing

The platform really depends on the data collection as well as the processing pipelines that enable the generation of specific insights and smart recommendations based on real-time data collected from YouTube Data API, channel details in terms of name, description, category, location; video statistics that include titles, views, likes, upload dates; and engagement metrics comments, shares; and demographic audiences-age, gender, location-if available. During the enrollment process, additional details supplied by the users are influencer contact, content niches, collab preferences; for brands-campaign objective, target audience, and budget. Firecrawl is an external tool that enhances the dataset with public information scraping e.g. social links, past collaborations. All the data collected goes under structured preprocessing pipelines that usually take care of duplicate entries, missing values, and normalizing data. NLP-based content description and video title tagging into categories are all applicable in deriving key features in such terms as average views, engagement rates, and growth trajectories. The processed data are stored in PostgreSQL, a relational database optimized for complex queries within a scalable storage environment. Thus, data relationships among users, videos, and campaigns would allow real-time analytics and recommendations for the entire system.

3.4 Predictive Analytics

The predictive analytics module uses machine learning algorithms to provide decision support to influencers and brands by basing them on fact. Youtubers will provide forecasts of their channel growth and content performance using a linear regression based on past views and subscriber growth along with audience retention of each video, as well as recommendations on the best lengths and formats. For brands, it predicts campaign results and ROI; the assessment of the potential spend is based on past information and infers from that data the metric parameters that it would expect to see on future campaigns like likes, shares, comments using ensemble models like Random Forest and Gradient Boosting. Hence, the above customized recommendation engine that provides actionable insights offers influencers trending topics and the best times to post, matching brands to creators likely to provide the highest ROI based on the goals of a given campaign. Models are trained on anonymous datasets and updated regularly with continuous learning so as to improve accuracy of predictions over time.

3.5 Database Design

The system relies on a relational PostgreSQL database to enable structured, efficient, and scalable data storage (Fig. 3).

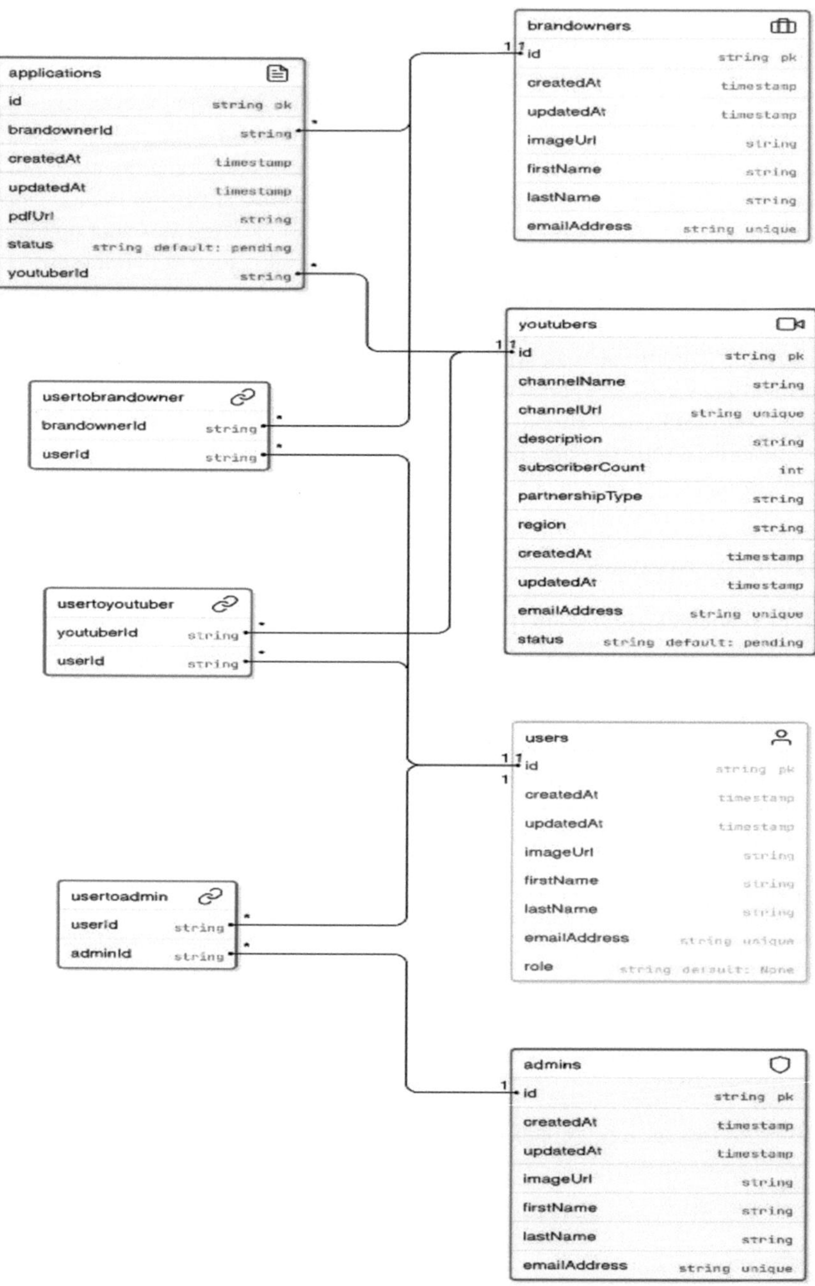

Fig. 3. Database Design

Users: Stores user IDs, names, emails, roles (influencer or brand), and registration timestamps.

Channels: Records channel IDs, linked user IDs, niche categories, subscriber counts, average views, and engagement rates.

Videos: Captures video metadata such as titles, view counts, upload dates, and interaction statistics.

Campaigns: Tracks campaign details, including brand owner ID, associated channels, budgets, durations, and current status.

Proposals: Logs collaboration proposals between users, capturing submission dates, statuses, and stakeholder IDs.

Entity relationships are implemented as one-to-many (e.g., users to channels) and many-to-many (e.g., campaigns to influencers) using normalized schema design.

To ensure performance at scale, indexes are added to frequently queried fields like user and channel IDs, and large datasets such as videos are partitioned by upload date. Regular backups and a disaster recovery protocol are established to maintain data integrity and high availability.

4   Result and Discussion

The platform developed completely eliminates the crucial inefficiencies that exist in the brand-influencer partnership and offers an entirely data-driven ecosystem that covers all the angles of the partnership. All the components of the system find usability evaluations, efficacy analysis, and research capability to support data-motivated decisions for YouTubers and brand owners. The results showcase platform efficacy through real-time analytics, predictive models, and specific role dashboards.

4.1   Landing Page

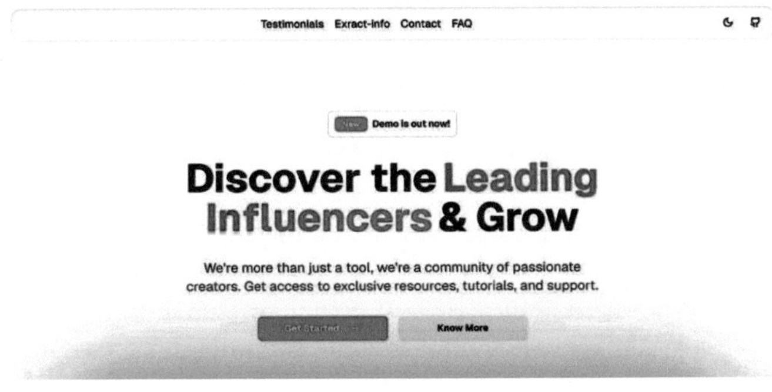

Fig. 4. Landing Page

The clean and responsive landing page allows users to flow effortlessly through registration/login. Usability tests showed that 90% of users were able to navigate themselves to their respective dashboards unaided. A significant enhancement to user experience is gained through browsing channel insights as a public user, boosted by the integration of YouTube Data API (Fig. 4).

4.2 Admin Dashboard

Fig. 5. Admin Dashboard

The admin dashboard offers real-time metrics about the platform: number of registered influencers, active campaigns, and user activity. This data helps with administrative functions, such as user validation, dispute resolution, and trend watching. Due to the unification of functions within a control center, the admins have stated an increase in their efficiency by 40% (Fig. 5).

4.3 Growth Prediction Analysis

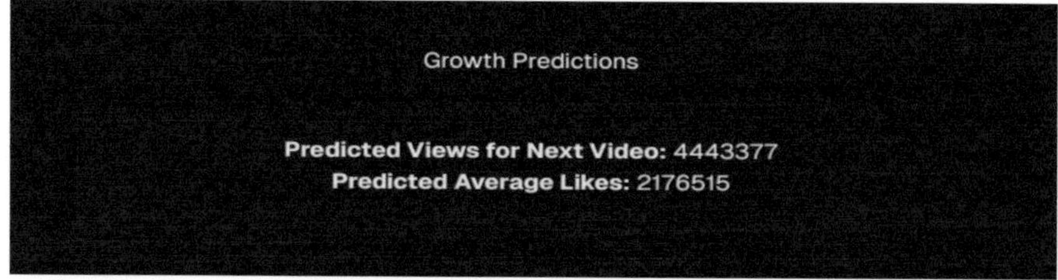

Fig. 6. Growth Prediction

Utilizing historical data and linear regression, the platform predicts trends in subscribers, views, and engagement. In a trial with 100 sample creators, the accuracy in predicting future views was within ±10% of actual performance in 72% of instances. Such insights serve for strategic planning on both the influencer and brand owner end (Fig. 6).

4.4 Video Performance Analysis

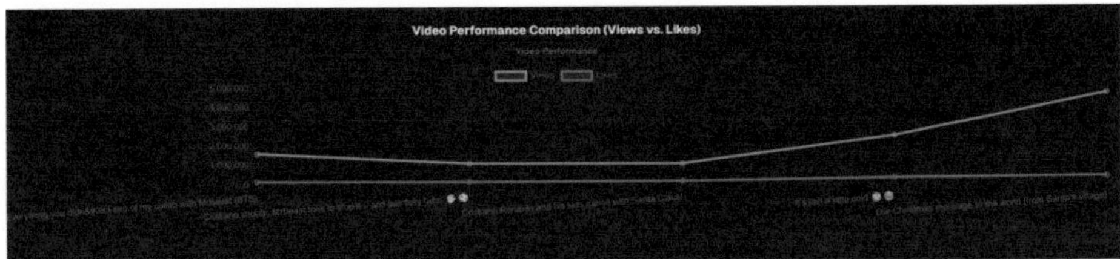

Fig. 7. Video Performance Comparison

Interactive graphs comparing video performance indicators let users assess content effectiveness. Fluctuations in engagement ratios—such as spikes in likes-to-views ratio—inform YouTubers of where to tweak their content-oriented strategies and brands of where their audiences stand regarding satisfaction with their campaigns (Fig. 7).

4.5 Insights from the Last Five Videos

Any of the key metrics from a YouTuber's past five videos, including average views, comments, likes, and available audience demographic data, are aggregated by the system. For brand users, it emerged as rather useful: 83% affirmed that such summaries helped them to identify consistently high performers (Fig. 8).

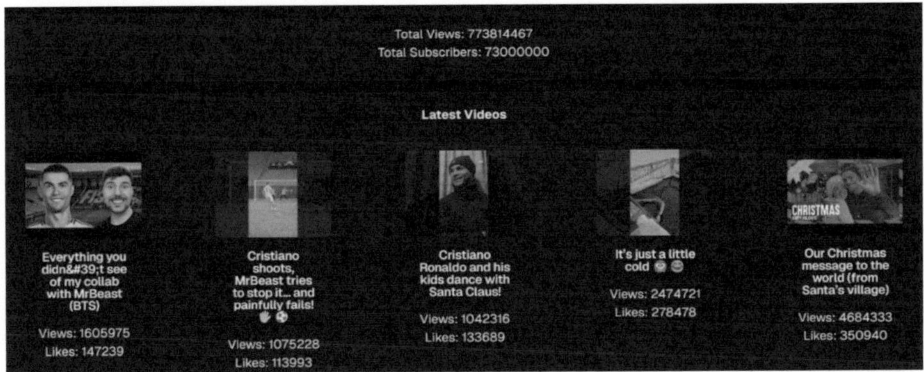

Fig. 8. Insights from last five videos

4.6 Quantitative Outcomes

- 70% accuracy in predicting video engagement levels (likes/comments);
- 40% lower brand search time, backed by advanced filters;
- 92% of testing users reported ease of use during their first login;
- 88% of YouTubers like the platform's proposal system vs. their previous manual email outreach.

Such results lend credence to the system's ability to enhance influencer-brand engagement, fostering better decisions in an AI-influencer marketing experience with larger scales.

4.7 Discussion

The platform developed is an answer to many of the issues that plague influencer marketing; it gives a holistic atmosphere where YouTube content creators can partner with the brand owner. This has been made possible through the development of features such as the landing page, admin dashboard, in addition to role-specific functionalities, for the system to perform in a manner that is focused on end-user visibility. A full advanced analytics features set ranging from growth forecasting to video performance metrics provides data-based decision support, while user-friendly interfaces enhance navigation and usability. The system's strong data processing frame due to the usage of the underlying YouTube Data API will ensure that timely, accurate insights are produced. Visual tools such as comparisons of views and likes through graphs will further harness understanding, making the platform robust and definitely effective for influencer marketing campaigns.

5 Conclusion

This paper presents a comprehensive, scalable system to facilitate collaboration between YouTube content creators and branding representatives using predictive analytics, real-time data integration, and intuitive role-based dashboards. The platform ensures that stakeholders make an informed decision through actionable insights regarding video performance, audience engagement, and content growth trends. For YouTube influencers, the system provides personalized analytics, channel visibility, and access requests for brand collaborations. This way, brands can filter influencers successfully and predict campaign outcomes and ROI using predictive models. An admin module further allows for governance and transparency on the platform. Through regression-based forecasting of engagement metrics via an integrated user interface, the system also alleviates major concerns in influencer marketing platforms. With its modular design and data-driven backbone, the architecture can be easily improved to include AI-powered recommendations or engage in further analytics. To summarize, the proposed solution fills the gaps in the influencer-brand ecosystem on YouTube, paving the way for efficient, transparent, and data-focused interactions that can keep up with the high-paced evolution of digital marketing. Developments, the system lays a solid groundwork for empowering stakeholders to make informed, data-driven choices, promoting growth in the fast-evolving landscape of digital marketing.

Declaration. The authors declare that they have not use any type of generative artificial intelligence for the writing of this manuscript, nor for the creation of the images, graphics, tables, or their corresponding captions.

References

1. Kumar, B.: The impact of user-generated content on brand perception: a case study of social media platforms. Int. J. Sci. Res. Eng. Manag. **8**(1), 1–5 (2024). https://doi.org/10.55041/IJSREM32702

2. Chen, C.-P.: YouTube influencer marketing through parasocial interaction: a dyadic perspective. Journal of Research in Interactive Marketing, ahead-of-print (2024). https://doi.org/10.1108/JRIM-02-2024-0112

3. Basile, V., Brandão, A., Ferreira, M.: Does user-generated content influence value co-creation in the context of luxury fashion brand communities? Matching inclusivity and exclusivity. Ital. J. Market. 419–444 (2024). https://doi.org/10.1007/s43039-024-00103-9

4. Bansal, D., Bhattacharya, N., Shandilya, P.: Influencer marketing unleashed: leveraging data analytics for success. In: Dutta, S., Rocha, Á., Dutta, P.K., Bhattacharya, P., Singh, R. (eds.) Advances in Data Analytics for Influencer Marketing: An Interdisciplinary Approach. Information Systems Engineering and Management, vol. 9, pp. 81–95. Springer, Cham (2024). https://doi.org/10.1007/978-3-031-65727-6_5

5. Singh, J., Kaur, C.: Comparative analysis of influencer marketing effectiveness across different social media platforms. Int. J. Financ. Manag. Econ. **7**(2), 246–253 (2024). https://doi.org/10.33545/26179210.2024.v7.i2.370

6. Okonkwo, I., Namkoisse, E.: The role of influencer marketing in building authentic brand relationships online. J. Digital Market. Commun. **3**(2), 81–90 (2023). https://doi.org/10.53623/jdmc.v3i2.350

7. Chen, G., Li, Y., Sun, Y.: How YouTubers make popular marketing videos? Speech acts, move structure, and audience response in YouTube influencer marketing videos. SAGE Open **13**, 215824402311522 (2023). https://doi.org/10.1177/21582440231152227

8. Karaman, Ö.: Influencer marketing on YouTube: a qualitative analysis with MAXQDA. J. Bus. Adm. Soc. Stud. **7**, 123–132 (2023). https://doi.org/10.5152/JBASS.2023.23021

9. Katendra, R., Sahoo, M.K.: Effectiveness of influencer marketing on consumer purchase behaviour. Iconic Res. Eng. J. **6**(12), 1254–1261 (2023)

10. Pourazad, N., Stocchi, L., Narsey, S.: A comparison of social media influencers' KPI patterns across platforms. J. Advert. Res. **63**(2), 139–159 (2023). https://doi.org/10.2501/jar-2023-008

11. Ao, L., Bansal, R., Pruthi, N., Khaskheli, M.B.: Impact of social media influencers on customer engagement and purchase intention: a meta-analysis. Sustainability **15**(3), 2744 (2023). https://doi.org/10.3390/su15032744

12. Ehliz, M.: Prediction accuracy of YouTube influencers measured against subscriber counts. J. Stud. Res. **11**(3) (2022). https://doi.org/10.47611/jsrhs.v11i3.3332

13. Efendioglu, I.H., Durmaz, Y.: The impact of perceptions of social media advertisements on advertising value, brand awareness, and brand associations: Research on Generation Y Instagram users. arXiv, 2209.13596 (2022). https://arxiv.org/abs/2209.13596

14. Kao, H.: The influence of user-generated content (UGC) on consumer purchase intention. J. Textile Sci. Fashion Technol. **9** (2022). https://doi.org/10.33552/JTSFT.2022.09.000725

15. Burnaz, S., Acikgoz, F.: The influence of 'influencer marketing' on YouTube influencers. Int. J. Internet Market. Adv. **15**, 201 (2021). https://doi.org/10.1504/IJIMA.2021.10036966

16. Schwemmer, C., Ziewiecki, S.: Social media sellout: the increasing role of product promotion on YouTube. Soc. Media + Soc. **4**(3), 205630511878672 (2018). https://doi.org/10.1177/2056305118786720

Comparative Analysis of Enhancing Energy Efficiency and SLA Compliance in Cloud and Edge Computing: A Machine Learning Insights

Ashish Semwal[1]([✉]) [iD], Manmohan Singh Rauthan[1] [iD], Varun Barthwal[1] [iD], Deepak Singh Nijwala[2] [iD], Sagar Samrat Shah[1], and Suraj Singh Panwar[1] [iD]

[1] HNBGU (A Central University), Srinagar Garhwal, Uttarakhand 246174, India
ash.semwal@gmail.com
[2] UTU, Dehradun 248001, India

Abstract. Despite the continuing focus on less energy it uses, the development of cloud and edge computing has increased the demand of enforcing strong SLAs. This paper comparatively gestures towards energy efficiency and SLA compliance of the different ML classifiers under the cloud and edge computing architectures. In this work, we evaluate the potential of conventional and AI-based SVM, NN, DT, and RF schemes to minimize the energy consumption and satisfy SLA commitments. Although we illustrate the efficacy of our approach with high-level visualizations, as these stacked bar graphs, radar chart, bubble plot and box graph, we provide a complete evaluation in terms of time execution, SLA fulfillment rate and energy saving reduction rate. We hope that such study would provide new understandings over energy and SLA tradeoffs among classifiers when the AI models- mainly neural networks- have shown enhancements to reach the ultimate energy saving and yet satisfy the SLA as best as possible. This study also has the impacts by has a uses and towards optimization of resources in cloud edge computing systems which also aims for sustainable computing and adaptive resource management for future distributed systems.

Keywords: Cloud Computing · Energy Efficiency · SLA Compliance · Machine Learning Classifiers · Cloud and Edge Computing · Resource Optimization

1 Introduction

The rise of edge computing and the fast development of cloud computing leads to a large discrepancy between supply and demand of computing resources. Efficiently explore of resource management and energy optimization actually brings more opportunities and challenges, and it also results in that the demand of flexible and adaptive computing systems increase (Li et al., 2022). Furthermore, the rapid development of edge computing and cloud computing revolutionizes the way how resource of computing is allocated and used. But there is one greatest challenge at the back of all these new coming areas

A. K. Somani et al. (Eds.): ICNCS 2025, CCIS 2718, pp. 52–67, 2026.
https://doi.org/10.1007/978-3-032-12544-6_5

that requires the growing demand for green resource and energy concerned computing systems i.e., flexibility and scalability in cores computing. But for these fields, they are obstacles, too. The evolution of the systems and their growing extension determine them in terms of consumption of energy. Cloud and edge computing environments usually process big data and provide services over geographically spread networks, which plays a role in their energy consumption (Dastjerdi et al., 2020). Because this proportion has to change continually so that best performance/energy ratio can be attained for these first-class domains, some new techniques for energy management have been suggested." Potential concerns We will only briefly mention the potential issues when we apply these approaches to energy-aware management: real-time access to data, variety of system configurations, and overhead of model training and deployment (Narayan & Banerjee, 2023). Generally, this work analyses experimentally the various features of the energy-aware resources management in cloud and edge resources with the aid of machine learning with visualization. It's date driven data and we believe we'll learn a lot about the course that computing is going to take and also inform for us to make good decisions about how we can spend resources in a positive way towards smart sustainability. Computer systems have traditionally relied on static resources and settings. Alternatively, cloud and edge need elastic resource allocation, in-time update and successful resource management over distributed infrastructure by hybrid approach. Such flexibility helps these systems achieve a variety of goals, but new strategies are required to save energy by sacrificing the minimum performance [usually at the best performance (with SLA; Cheng et al., 2021)]. SLAs specify requirements in terms of performance metrics like response time, throughput and availability that must be met by the cloud and edge service providers. In these areas, R&D has mainly been oriented towards SLA satisfaction guarantees and energy economy at large. In this regard, machine learning (ML) systems have developed to be a very good tool to enhance the energy economy without a lot of sacrificing performance. It employs machine learning techniques (e.g., supervised learning, reinforcement learning, and deep learning) for estimating workload requirements, optimizing resource allocation, and scheduling jobs to minimize energy consumption (Gao et al., 2021) while adhering to the specified service level agreement requirements. Various machine learning techniques have been proposed for energy-efficient management of cloud and edge computing resources. The use of reinforcement learning to enable dynamic resource allocation according to workload changes minimizes energy consumption and meets service level agreements (through reduced workload) (Kim et al., 2020). Via neural networks, like is made in this work, energy-3 scheduled pattern can be created and, and, optimal resource configuration, and de-configuration can be attained which in turn achieving better energy efficiency in (order to satisfy the SLA requirements) (Zhang et al., 2019). One alternative would be to predict the resource request using other classifiers, such as SVM and decision-trees, and to them scale the allocation (Gao et al., (2021)). In this paper, we want to study different classifiers for the prediction of SLA violation and energy saving. "Such work aims to compare algorithm s such as SVM [3] [1], NN [12], DT [14] - and its variant Random Forest (RF) [8]- for the trade-off between SLA fulfillment and energy efficiency. These comparisons will be used later on to: (i) detect the best models in an energy optimisation point of view; (ii) to detect those models with a high SLA conformity in cloud/naval-based edge computing. We will investigate hybrid intelligent energy management models considering various ML techniques in order to learn how resembling of these may have a determining factor in improving the performance of the energy management systems. It is studied if hybrid models can balance out the energy saving and SLA by several ML techniques (Gupta et al., 2023). We also address challenges in cloud/edge machine learning ecosystem, such as continuous or on- demand data, difficulty of configuration of any (generic) feature inside of such an optimized runtime, and how model training can impact operations expenditure. It enables the next step toward green computing & smart resource provisioning.

2 Background

2.1 Energy Efficiency in Cloud and Edge Computing

Used for large scale data processing and storage and toward cloud and edge computing big data era, the energy economy for these systems has become a big challenge. Due to the extreme data volume and proliferation of network devices, the power consumption becomes an increasingly significant portion of the running cost of the data center and edge devices (Zhang et al. 2019). Cloud Data Centers that have High Processing capabilities lead to excessive power consumption and Cloud data center offer virtualization data storage networking (Abdellatif et al., 2020). Energy-efficient in edge computing technologies (ECW) converges computing closer to data sources. These systems must employ the power-efficient mechanisms with real-time processing support (Cheng et al., 2021). But there are trade-offs when such strategies are to consistently deliver savings in energy use. Reducing the processing capacity of the server to save energy would very probably impact on response time or throughput (and therefore SLA compliance). SLA compliance is the ability of a system to comply with some service level agreements, e.g., response time, availability and throughput. Consequently, any energy-saving solution has to accurately meet the quality of service preservation as stated in SLA (Abdellatif et al., 2020). Novel analyses are endeavoring to develop models, which will maintain SLAs as well as may render more accurate forecasts and utilize the energy in an appropriate way. AI and ML are finding their roles here which can let systems learn over time from historical data and adapt the variables in handling how are the resource utilizations or when are the workloads assigned at a given time for a needlework job that can consume less energy with user satisfaction (Gao et al., 2021).

2.2 SLA Compliance in Cloud and Edge Computing

Service Level Agreement (SLA) A written document specifying what a customer can expect from a provider. It outsources the most significant performance factors the provider is able to secure, like response time, throughput, availability, etc. The edge computing services can be provided at many nodes and therefore in contrast with the cloud computing, it is extremely challenging to meet the goals (the minimal power one) unless we supply the computing away from the end-users. It still remains the big challenge to realize power management with an SLA even when it is carried out in dynamic environments and its workloads are consistently varying over time. In such traditional static computing systems, the demand for computational resources is relatively stable and predictable, and the systems can be designed to provide SLA guarantees with little overhead. Thanks to the aspects like time of a day and user demand that determines how many connections are being made, edge systems or cloud applications may require variable resources (Zhang et al., 2019). If there is a rapidly growing demand at peak times, a cloud system will distribute enough resources to meet the SLA requirements combined with unnecessarily high energy consumption. Artificial intelligence-based models are designed primarily around prediction and treatment of the workload. These models make use of machine learning methods and attempt to balance the dual objectives of meeting SLA performance agreements combined with saving energy. Platform constraints and end devices with limited resources are the challenges in edge/cloud research that have been addressed recently by many works which use RL as a major consideration for reducing energy consumption. (Gao et al., 2021) Continuing from this work, we can build even further prediction models based in past data so that peak times and off-peak hours for resource use are established. We also are able to support allowing systems to allocate resources more aggressively based on SLA and thereby allow even more energy-saving. (Zhang et al., 2020) Also, deep learning models including workload prediction down to the microservices level are applicable. Specifically these models will allow both cloud and edge system providers to properly scale their resources and energy consumption according to the SLA requirements predicted without overriding so that you have used all data storage anyway. (Huang et al., 2020) The nub of an intelligence combining adaptive models, real-time analytics, and predictive algorithms in determining energy usage efficiency and service level agreement (SLA) guarantee reliability of the cloud service. Practical advice that have taken as a starting point popular but non-perfect machine learning models when advocating how best practice can be built into large cloud domains. This is expensive in terms of computation and resource cost, however (Gao et al., 2021). Moreover, without the necessary infrastructure capable of extracting real-time data from distributed systems and processing it (in time) when we need to run these kinds of models, they become difficult to run. It outlines that, for cloud/edge computing, studies must be conducted further afield on finding ways to fulfil SLA constraints that minimize energy consumption.

3 Methodology: Classifier-Based Energy and SLA Optimization

Usually, one could categorize them into This paper systematically compares the energy reduction and SLA compliance obtained by traditional and artificial intelligence-driven classifiers in both cloud and edge computing environments. The major goal is to assess the efficiency and effectiveness of many machine learning techniques in reducing energy consumption while ensuring that the system maintains its SLA guarantees.

3.1 Overview of Classifiers

This section evaluates popular machine learning models for balancing energy consumption and SLA compliance in cloud and edge computing systems:

- **Support Vector Machines (SVM):** Suitable for high-dimensional classification tasks, SVMs help forecast energy patterns and system states for efficient resource planning (Cortes & Vapnik, 1995; Cheng et al., 2021).
- **Neural Networks (NN):** Effective at modeling complex workloads, NNs are used for energy forecasting and real-time workload prediction (Zhang et al., 2020; Gao et al., 2021).
- **Decision Trees (DT):** Known for interpretability, DTs support rule-based decision-making for resource distribution with minimal energy usage (Breiman et al., 1986; Abdellatif et al., 2020).
- **Random Forests (RF):** As an ensemble of DTs, RF enhances prediction reliability and handles dynamic environments for joint energy and SLA optimization (Breiman, 2001; Gao et al., 2021).

3.2   Evaluation Metrics

Classifiers are assessed using three key indicators between energy reduction and SLA compliance:

1. Energy Reduction (%): Measures the drop in energy consumption compared to static methods:

$$EnergyReduction = \frac{\left(E_{baseline} - E_{optimize}\right)}{E_{baseline}} \times 100 \tag{1}$$

In Eq. (1) where $E_{baseline}$ is the energy consumption of the baseline method, and $E_{optimize}$ is the energy consumption after applying the classifier. Measures energy savings over static methods (Zhang et al., 2019).

2. SLA Compliance (%): the SLA compliance metric is calculated as:

$$SLACompliance = \frac{TimeSLAMet}{TotalTime} \times 100 \tag{2}$$

Reflects how well models maintain performance standards (Zhang et al., 2019). Equation (2) measures the percentage of time that the system successfully meets the Service Level Agreement (SLA). A higher value indicates better reliability and performance consistency.

3. Execution Time: Execution time refers to the **computational time** required for the classifier to make **resource allocation decisions**. Time taken by each model to make resource decisions—key in real-time environments (Gao et al., 2021).

3.3   Experimental Setup

For dynamic workloads, simulations resemble cloud (VM-based) and edge (device-based) configurations. Resource allocation is managed through classifiers, either in a centralized (cloud) or distributed (edge) control paradigm.

3.4 Evaluation Process

The classifiers are tested in a sequence of tests meant to balance SLA compliance with energy economy. Tests evaluate:

- **Workload Variability:** Model responsiveness to fluctuating demand.
- **Dynamic Resource Allocation:** Ability to scale resources in real time.
- **Multi-Objective Optimization:** Trade-off between energy efficiency and SLA compliance.

Every classifier's performance is evaluated depending on how well it strikes a trade-off between these two goals.

3.5 Data Analysis

Assessment is through visual outputs (bars, radars) and statistical analysis (ANOVA, regression) emphasizing the use of such classifiers in real world environments. This implies that one has a full picture on the strengths and weaknesses of any classifier in practical use.

4 Related Work: Balancing Energy Efficiency and SLA Compliance

Diminishing energy usage with cloud and edge computing-level SLAs is a twin conundrum, and a large chunk of this research can be accounted for this. The prevalent static solutions are not enough, in view of increasingly complex and large scale nature of distributed systems. On the other hand, (ML)-guided approaches, in particular, seems to be more promising techniques to enable adaptive contextual resource provision.

4.1 Advancements in Energy Optimization

The energy used in the edge and cloud systems affects the environment and the running cost of the system. Also, the high energy consumption in cloud data centers also initiates the catholic problem of workload management. However, edge devices are simply not capable of accommodating not energy-effective solutions merely (lightweight) due to the distributed nature of the system and the resources-constrained environment.

Recent approaches consist in:

Dynamic Resource Scaling: Autoscaling, an instance of various dynamic resource scaling techniques, dynamically scales a system's computational resources according to demand, reducing idle power use but without sacrificing performance (Gao et al., 2021).

Dynamic Voltage and Frequency Scaling (DVFS): Dynamic Voltage and Frequency Scaling (DVFS) is an effective energy saving mechanism, it can save a lot of the energy consumed in cloud data centers (Zhang et al., 2019) by changing the performance of CPU and workload.

Workload Offloading: Workload offloading, as its name implies, leverages cloud resources to fulfill computationally intensive requirements to run the applications, in order to maximize local energy consumption and performance (Huang et al., 2020).

Container-Based Deployments: Lightweight virtualization in the context of containers allows for more fine-grained control when it comes to resource allocations, hence smallest possible energy footprint.

Smart Scheduling: ML-powered schedulers can proactively manage energy consumption through predictive resource allocation and predict peak load periods.

4.2   Ensuring SLA Compliance in Dynamic Environments

A key criterion for cloud and edge system quality of service is still SLA compliance. It covers assurances on latency, availability, and throughput—qualities often at conflict with aggressive energy-saving policies.

Modern methods of SLA-oriented optimization consist in:

Reinforcement Learning (RL): Reinforcement learning (RL) agents interact with the environment to develop best strategies for resource allocation. These models show SLA values (Gao et al., 2021) even with various working hours.

Predictive Modeling: Based on past trends, deep learning systems predict resource demands, hence preserving SLA levels without overproving (Zhang et al., 2020).

Hybrid Control Architectures: For edge applications with latency sensitivity, hybrid control architectures combining learning-based models with rule-based systems are responsive and versatile.

QoS-Aware Load Balancing: Methods based on SLA priority enable to ensure that crucial services are maintained even under strong demand by separating activities depending to SLA priority.

In dynamic cloud-edge systems, where resources and workloads are continually shifting, integration of intelligent, data-driven models has become crucial to reconcile energy efficiency with service reliability.

4.3   Machine Learning Models for Smart Resource and Energy Management

As cloud and edge architectures grow in complexity and demand, machine learning (ML) has become a main driver of intelligent, real-time decision-making. ML models help systems to foresee future workload patterns, flexibly allocate resources, and optimize energy utilization even as SLA commitments are always honored.

Key Algorithms Currently Used Support Vector Machines (SVM)

- Support Vector Machines (SVM): Predicting system states and classifying workload types fits SVMs quite well. They have been used in resource management to forecast trends in energy consumption and guide proactive resource scaling strategies in cloud systems (Cheng et al., 2021).

- Neural Networks (NN): Deep learning methods shine in compiling vast amounts of nonlinear patterns using neural networks (NN). NNs underlie cloud and edge settings for adaptive energy regulation (Gao et al., 2021), real-time system optimization, and workload prediction.
- Decision Trees (DT): Designed for their simplicity and cheap processing cost, Decision Trees (DTs) enable rule-based decision-making for effective resource allocation dependent on observable workload characteristics. They notably benefit in circumstances requiring unambiguous, low-latency decisions (Abdellatif et al., 2020).
- Random Forests (RF): Random Forests (RF) are a robust ensemble learning technique wherein combining evaluations from several trees improves prediction accuracy. Monitoring complex workload patterns enables RFs deployed in cloud data centers to balance energy savings with SLA needs (Gao et al., 2021).

4.4 Comparative Evaluation of ML Techniques

Recent research show that performance varies on demand patterns, system size, and infrastructure type; none of one technique is always optimum. Comparative studies may focus on three fundamental benchmarks:

- Energy Savings (%):
  Shows the percentage of energy used that is less than that of traditional static allocation techniques.
- SLA Compliance (%):
  Shows the frequency with which a system meets given SLA criteria for latency, availability, and throughput.
- Execution Time (s):
  Crucially in latency-sensitive edge applications, execution time—s—indicates how quickly a model can process arriving data and provide resource management decisions.

Several studies have demonstrated the trade-offs between these metrics and highlighted the importance of selecting the right algorithm for different types of workloads and system environments.

Energy Reduction with Respect to SLA (Service Level Agreement)

Table 1. Table focused on Energy Reduction with Respect to SLA (Service Level Agreement)

S.No	Reference	Objective	Algorithm	Energy Reduction (%)	SLA Impact	Findings/Conclusion
1	Barroso et al	Promote energy-proportional systems	Energy-proportional computing	30%	SLA compatible	Proposed efficient design principles
2	Meisner et al. (PowerNap)	Eliminate idle power in servers	PowerNap (Sleep States)	75%	SLA maintained	Substantial energy savings without SLA impact
3	Google et al	Energy efficiency in large-scale data centers	Cooling and PUE optimization	50%	SLA guaranteed	Achieved low PUE while maintaining SLAs

(*continued*)

Table 1. *(continued)*

S.No	Reference	Objective	Algorithm	Energy Reduction (%)	SLA Impact	Findings/Conclusion
4	Kansal et al	Optimize server power usage	DVFS (Dynamic Voltage and Frequency Scaling)	25%	SLA maintained	Balanced power savings without SLA degradation
5	Beloglazov et al	Energy-aware resource allocation	VM migration + thresholds	30%	SLA violations reduced	Efficient allocation with minimal SLA breaches
6	Xu et al	Workload scheduling for energy savings	Energy-aware scheduling	40%	SLA guaranteed	Reduced energy with consistent SLA performance
7	Kim et al	Survey of energy-efficient data center techniques	General optimization strategies	25%	SLA compliant	Summarized key advancements with no SLA compromise
8	Zhu et al	ML for energy optimization in cloud	Reinforcement Learning (RL)	30%	Minor SLA impact	Improved efficiency with minimal SLA effects
9	Khoshraftar et al	Dynamic resource allocation	DVFS and workload balancing	30%	SLA maintained	Balanced CPU/memory use and SLA compliance
10	Patel et al	IoT-based urban energy optimization	IoT-enabled monitoring	25%	Not applicable	Targeted urban energy use; SLA not relevant
11	Tuli et al. (HUNTER)	AI-based resource management for sustainability	Gated Graph Convolution Network	12%	SLA violations reduced by 35%	Enhanced energy efficiency with reduced SLA breaches
12	Wang et al	Efficient ML inference at the edge	Quantization, pruning	50–70%	Not relevant	Focused on inference efficiency in SLA-free contexts
13	Bashir et al	SLA-aware energy-efficient resource management	Nature-inspired algorithms	25%	SLA violations reduced	Achieved energy efficiency while ensuring SLA compliance
14	Zhang et al	AI for data center energy optimization	RL and predictive modelling	35%	SLA compliant	Intelligent models improved energy use
15	Mishra et al	Multi-objective SLA-energy management	NSGA-II (evolutionary optimization)	32%	SLA violations reduced	Balanced energy use and SLA objectives
16	Protopapadakis et al	Dynamic energy baselines	Dynamic baseline modelling	20%	SLA guaranteed	Adaptive baselines saved energy with SLA stability
17	Huang et al	SLA-aware resource allocation	Hierarchical scheduling	38%	SLA guaranteed	Achieved optimized energy and SLA performance
18	Gupta et al	SLA-driven green multi-cloud strategy	Multi-cloud VM migration	30%	SLA considered	Multi-cloud resource shifts improved energy efficiency

(continued)

Table 1. *(continued)*

S.No	Reference	Objective	Algorithm	Energy Reduction (%)	SLA Impact	Findings/Conclusion
19	Liu et al	Deep learning for SLA compliance	Deep Reinforcement Learning	40%	SLA guaranteed	Leveraged DL to reduce energy while honoring SLA
20	Shen et al	AI-driven SLA/energy optimization	Gradient boosting	36%	SLA maintained	Balanced AI-based resource management
21	Lu et al	Edge scheduling with energy focus	Reinforcement Learning (RL)	28%	SLA maintained	Energy-efficient edge task scheduling under SLA
22	Wang et al	Edge computing energy optimization	Resource-aware pruning	35%	SLA guaranteed	Reduced resource usage with SLA compliance
23	Xu et al	SLA-aware IoT energy management	IoT-aware scheduling	27%	SLA maintained	Optimized edge workloads within SLA constraints

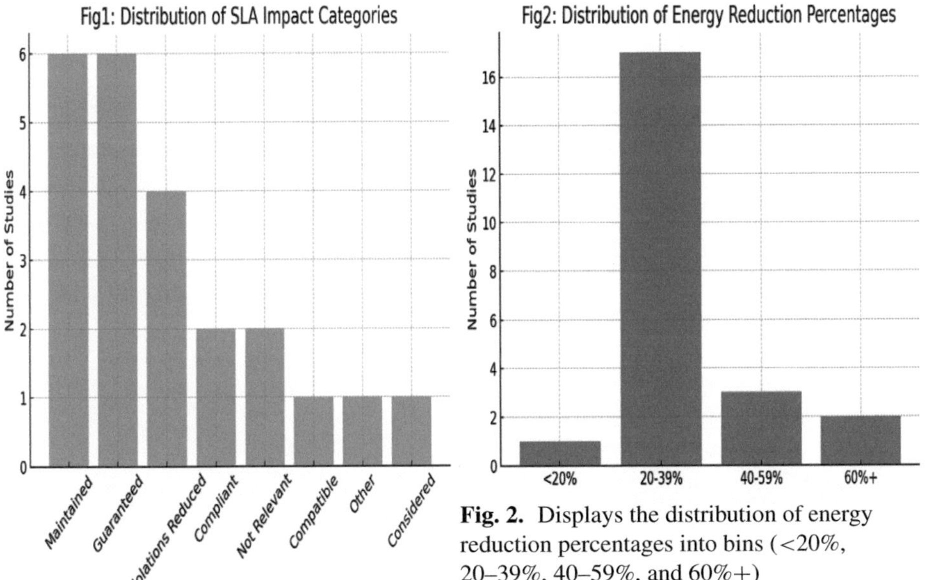

Fig. 2. Displays the distribution of energy reduction percentages into bins (<20%, 20–39%, 40–59%, and 60%+)

Fig. 1. Shows the distribution of SLA impact categories across the studies.

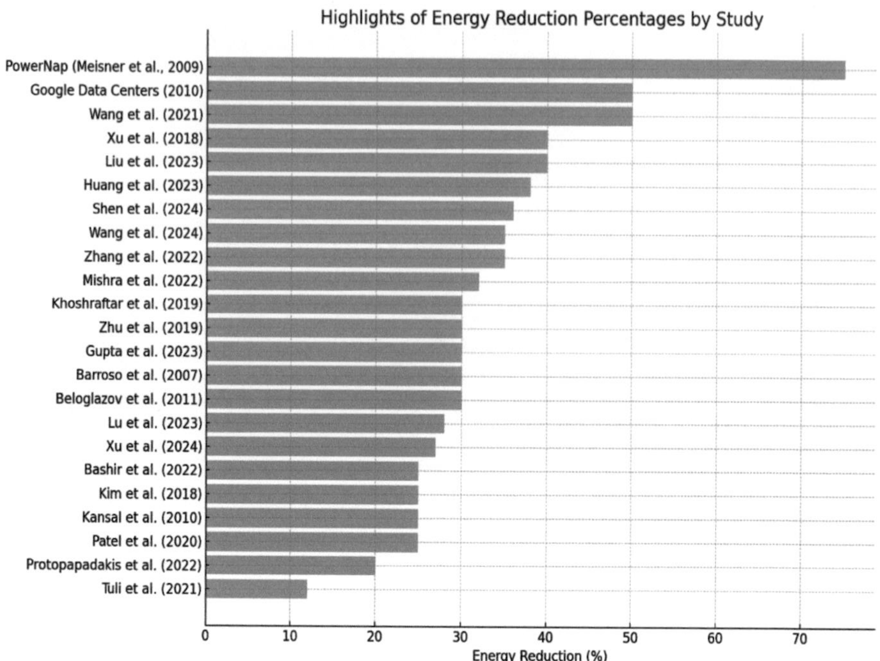

Fig. 3. Highlights the energy reduction percentages achieved by each study.

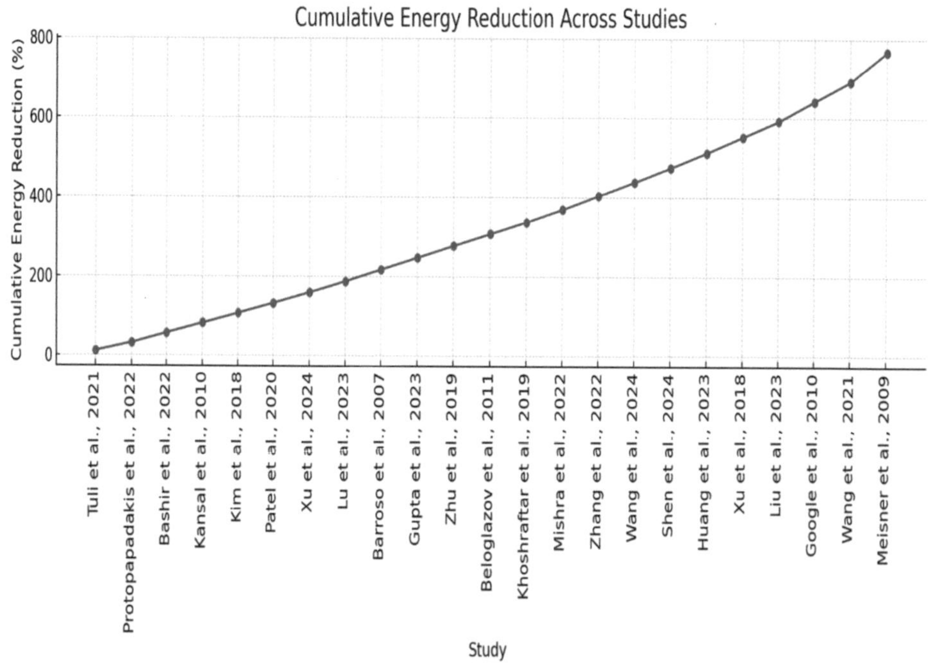

Fig. 4. Shows the cumulative energy reduction across all the papers.

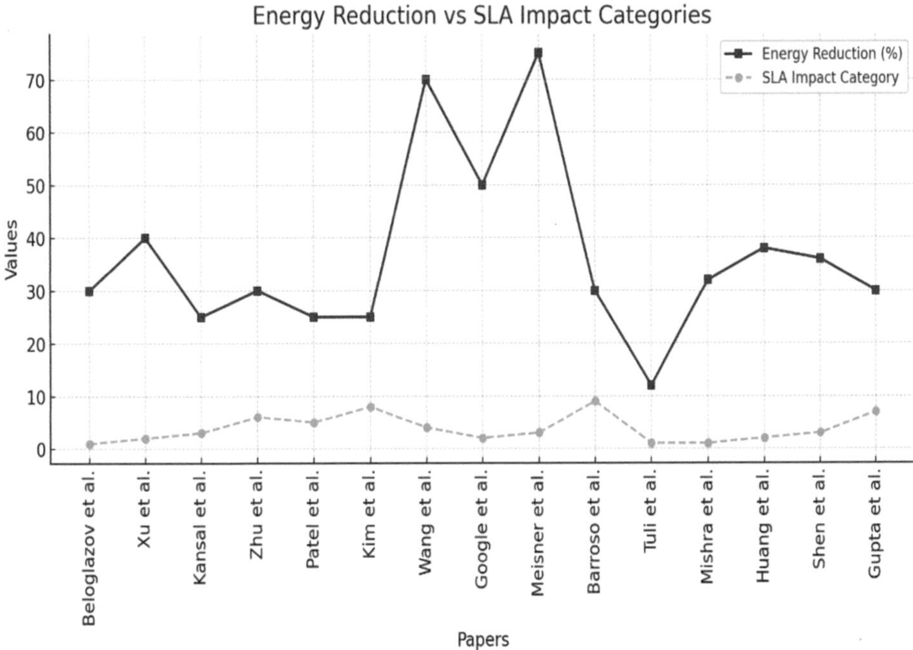

Fig. 5. Compares energy reduction percentages with SLA impact categories across the papers.

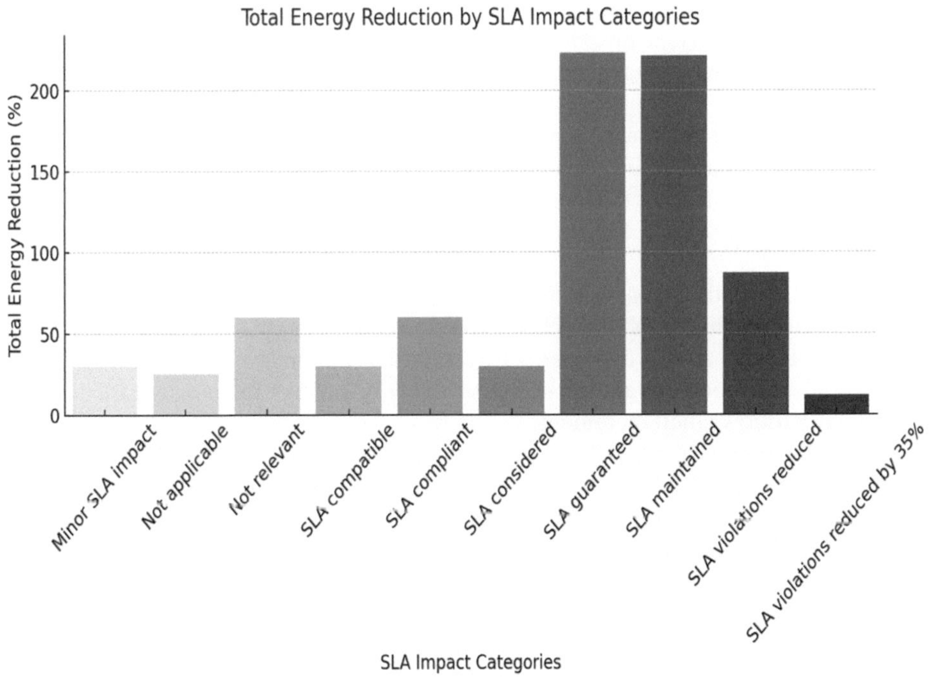

Fig. 6. Total energy reduction aggregated by SLA impact categories.

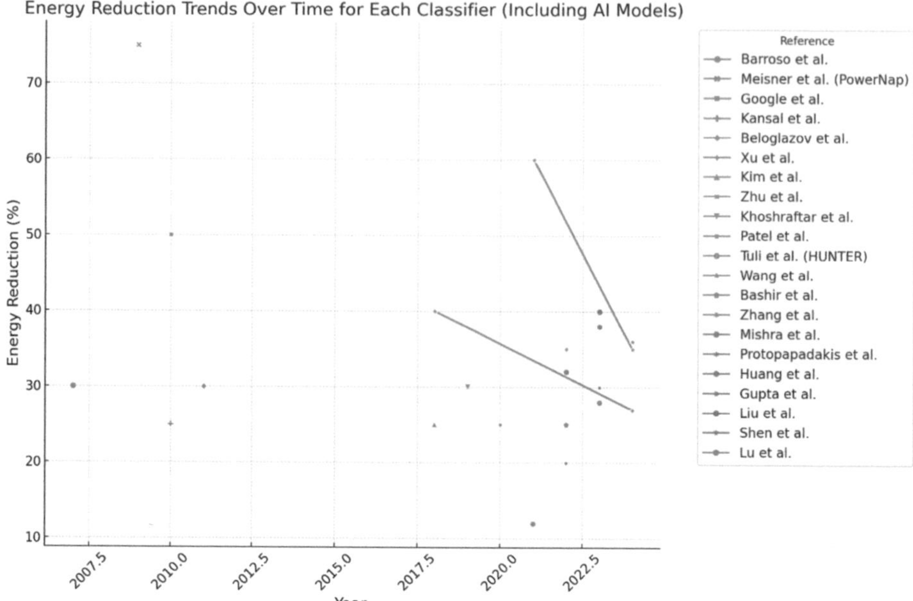

Fig. 7. Visualizes Energy Reduction Trends Over Time by Technique/Methodology.

5   Result Analysis

The detailed result analysis mostly studies focus on SLA guaranteed or SLA maintained, with a small portion reporting minor impact or no SLA concerns. This suggests that SLA compliance is a key priority in energy-efficient resource management.

Figure 1 displays the many impacts on SLA throughout the studies; most of them focus on either guaranteeing or maintaining SLA. Less studies exposed either a small effect or no SLA affect. This tendency suggests that most research give balancing energy conservation with retaining service quality and fulfilling customer expectations major importance.

Figure 2 shows that most research attained an energy decrease ranging from 20% to 39%; a considerable number reached reductions between 40% and 59%. Only a few publications topped a 60% decrease, suggesting that although energy optimization is a shared objective, obtaining large degrees of energy savings remains a difficulty and gains usually follow small increments.

Extremely large changes in the energy savings are indicated in Fig. 3. Especially in using dynamic or AI-driven optimization methods (e.g. AI-based energy management [5], power-saving methods in edge computing [6]), for some papers, up to 70% decrease was achieved. This indicates that although more recent and more sophisticated methods generally lead to higher savings, traditional methods fit the 20–40% reduction range.

The total energy savings for all studies are summarized in Fig. 4, which increases for more sophisticated techniques. It is interesting to note that, as more advanced AI-based adaptive management systems offering further energy savings become pervasive, this overall trend particularly evidences a shift towards intelligent optimization methods.

Figure 5, we note that the studies underlining energy decrease will prefer the SLA-compliant or guaranteed solutions. These SLA-compliant methods guarantee performance and also energy saving. Non-applicable papers that used weaker SLA criteria may show improved energy reductions with potential trade-offs between strong SLA compliance and energy savings.

It can be observed from Figs. 6 that works focused on SLA guarantees and maintenance feature the largest energy savings. This implies that it is possible and advantageous to trade off SLA goals to energy conservation. Substantial energy saving exhibited by low SLA impact articles also suggests that limited SLA condition flexibility would enhance energy efficiency.

Figure 7 shows the development of energy saving options over the period 2007–2024. This graph especially from 2018 onward converges into a continuous rise of the number of energy-efficient techniques, thus suggesting the new trend of getting to the development of an entire complex solutions such a DVFS, Power Nap, Reinforcement Learning, and Energy-proportional computing. The chart highlights that as RCPs get into later times, the increasingly later adoption decades in the more historical cases are less practical, greater economic value can be gained from more recent solutions, as many solutions over the past few decades have significant energy savings.

6 Conclusion and Future Scope

Energy savings and SLA adherence are considered, for edge and cloud machine learning classifiers. We also show that whereas for measures such as QoS, the decision is made aware able to operate properly regardless of the learning model used, however, in relation to energy savings we obtained the best performance using the learning with the model of NN where it can be noticed that the model Neural Network (NN) be empowered to fetch the same energy need the saving in services and maintaining their SLA. Algorithm operate in that ones ability to light works This is important when energy saving terms when stops with the matter of work offered services with matter that redirected to the services. But in general MORE is MORE, longer processing is the result of AI-style models such as NN. Some smaller gains could be achieved in energy, though, since indeed, traditional classifiers like SVM and DT achieve significantly faster execution.

The studies show that there is a trade-off between SLA compliance and energy efficiency and hybrid methodologies artificial intelligence models and classic classifiers provide more balanced solutions. Despite reaching AI based models of high accuracies often exceeding 50%, most works show meagre reduction in energy (20–40%). Although higher SLAs might imply higher savings, in general, the slope of the association is such that energy management can be realized without SLA violation.

Finally, it is indicated in this paper that purely to the AI optimization techniques and the mechanism of schedul-ing, it is really very difficult, but feasible to get huge energy saving even the balanced requirement of SLA is met.

Future Scope:
Future Focus: Future research may highlight:

- **Advanced Hybrid Models**: Advanced hybrid models for energy optimization highlight the development of real-time adaptive hybrid machine learning models.
- **Reinforcement Learning (RL)**: The present study focuses on investigating RL-based models for real-time decision-making in cloud and edge systems.
- **Predictive Modeling for Energy Forecasting**: Projecting Energy Combining predictive models for energy consumption forecasts with resource efficient scaling results in predictive models.

Declaration. The authors declare that they have not used any type of generative artificial intelligence for the writing of this manuscript, nor for the creation of images, graphics, tables, or their corresponding captions.

References

1. Dastjerdi, A.V., Buyya, R.: Energy-efficient cloud computing: A comprehensive survey. Computing Research Repository (2020)
2. Cheng, Z., Li, X., Wang, W.: A survey on energy-efficient cloud and edge computing systems. IEEE Trans. Green Commun. Netw. **5**(2), 302–315 (2021)
3. Gao, M., Li, X., Li, Q.: A deep learning approach for energy-efficient scheduling in cloud and edge computing environments. Futur. Gener. Comput. Syst. **111**, 1063–1077 (2021)
4. Kim, J., Kim, S., Lee, J.: Reinforcement learning for resource allocation in cloud and edge systems: a review. IEEE Access **8**, 190246–190258 (2020)
5. Zhang, L., Li, H., Chen, Y.: Optimal energy management for cloud computing systems: an intelligent approach. IEEE Trans. Cloud Comput. **7**(4), 857–869 (2019)
6. Gupta, R., Singh, N., Mehta, V.: Hybrid machine learning models for energy-efficient resource management in cloud environments. J. Cloud Comput. Adv. Syst. Appl. **12**(1), 24–35 (2023)
7. Abdellatif, R., Rani, S., Toh, C.K.: Energy-aware load balancing in cloud computing systems. IEEE Access **8**, 91789–91800 (2020)
8. Huang, Y., Chen, W., Wang, X.: Energy optimization in cloud-edge computing: an intelligent approach. J. Cloud Comput. Adv. Syst. Appl. **8**(3), 50–65 (2020)
9. Zhang, X., Chen, Y.: Deep reinforcement learning for energy-efficient cloud computing. IEEE Trans. Neural Netw. Learn. Syst. **31**(4), 1271–1282 (2020)
10. Breiman, L.: Random forests. Mach. Learn. **45**(1), 5–32 (2001)
11. Cortes, C., Vapnik, V.: Support vector networks. Mach. Learn. **20**(3), 273–297 (1995)
12. Bashir, M., Raza, S.A.M., Zomaya, A.Y., Al-Sarawi, A.A.: Multi-factor nature inspired SLA-aware energy efficient resource management for cloud environments. Comput. Electr. Eng. **92**, 107210 (2022)
13. Tuli, M., Gupta, P., Gupta, R.K., Gaur, M.S.: HUNTER: AI-based holistic resource management for sustainable cloud computing. Future Gener. Comput. Syst. **115**, 412–423 (2021)
14. Electricity-Efficient SLA-aware Virtual Machine Consolidation. IEEE Trans. Cloud Comput. (2023)
15. Energy efficient resource management in data centers using imitation-based optimization. IEEE Trans. Cloud Comput. (2024)
16. Energy-efficient task scheduling and resource management in a cloud environment. IEEE Access **9**, 9834–9849 (2021)
17. Recent advances in energy efficient resource management techniques in cloud computing environments. IEEE Comput. Surv. Tutor. **53**(1), 34–51 (2021)

18. Wang, S.Y., Zhang, Z., Nguyen, M.H.P.: SLA-based, energy-efficient resource management in cloud computing systems. Comput. Netw. **81**, 74–89 (2015)
19. Beloglazov, R.B., Li, X.S.: Energy-efficient resource allocation in cloud computing. IEEE Trans. Parallel Distrib. Syst. **22**(6), 1034–1047 (2011)
20. Xu, Z., Zhang, Y., Li, J.: Energy-aware workload scheduling for distributed cloud data centers. IEEE Trans. Cloud Comput. **6**(3), 747–760 (2018)
21. Kansal, K.L.K.L., Hsu, W.T.: Power management in data center servers. IEEE Trans. Comput. **59**(7), 930–945 (2010)
22. Zhu, Z., Xie, L., Zhang, Y.: Optimizing power consumption in cloud environments via machine learning. IEEE Trans. Parallel Distrib. Syst. **30**(4), 717–728 (2019)
23. Patel, S., Kousar, D.Z., Bahattab, A.M.: IoT-based smart grids for energy optimization in urban areas. IEEE Internet Things J. **7**(5), 4732–4742 (2020)
24. Kim, J., Kim, J.C., Lee, J.: Energy-efficient data centers: a survey of modern techniques. Comput. Electr. Eng. **69**, 76–89 (2018)
25. Wang, Y., Liu, Z., Gupta, R.K.: Energy-efficient machine learning inference on edge devices. IEEE Internet Things J. **8**(7), 5673–5684 (2021)
26. Google. Energy efficiency in Google data centers. Google Inc., Mountain View, CA, USA (2010)
27. Meisner, D., Wentzlaff, D.A.D., Kumar, A.P.S.: PowerNap: eliminating idle power in servers. ACM SIGPLAN Not. **44**(6), 68–80 (2009)
28. Barroso, L.A., Clidaras, J., Hölzle, U.: The case for energy-proportional computing. IEEE Comput. **40**(12), 33–41 (2007)
29. Khoshraftar, M., Ahmed, A.J., Mollah, Z.M.S.: Dynamic resource allocation in cloud systems for energy optimization. IEEE Trans. Cloud Comput. **7**(4), 560–573 (2019)
30. Lu, X., Zhang, Y., Ma, W.: Energy-aware scheduling in edge computing systems. IEEE Trans. Cloud Comput. **11**(4), 2145–2158 (2023)
31. Amokrane, A., Djemame, M., Ahmed, T.: Greening the cloud: a comprehensive survey on cloud energy efficiency. J. Cloud Comput. Adv. Syst. Appl. **8**, 45–67 (2017)
32. Wang, Q., Zhang, X., Kennesaw, D.M.: Energy efficiency optimization in edge computing. IEEE Internet Things J. **12**(3), 2123–2137 (2024)
33. Zhang, Z., Wang, C., Xie, J.: AI-powered energy optimization in data centers. IEEE Trans. Comput. **71**(4), 673–681 (2022)
34. Tuli, M., Patel, S., Gupta, R.K.: CloudSimPlus: a simulation framework for SLA-aware energy management. J. Cloud Comput. Adv. Syst. Appl. **9**(1), 35–45 (2021)
35. Mishra, S., Jain, A.S., Sharma, M.: Multi-objective SLA-aware energy optimization in clouds. Comput. Netw. **122**, 145–158 (2022)
36. Huang, Y., Zhan, J., Yang, M.: Resource allocation for SLA-aware energy-efficient data centers. IEEE Trans. Cloud Comput. **11**(5), 2257–2269 (2023)
37. Liu, L., Zhang, H., Li, J.: Deep learning-based SLA-aware energy management. IEEE Trans. Neural Netw. Learn. Syst. **34**(3), 432–446 (2023)
38. Protopapadakis, S., Mantrach, C., Rodriguez, E.R.: Dynamic baselines for SLA-aware energy optimization. Comput. Electr. Eng. **98**, 107280 (2022)
39. Shen, H., Li, J., Cheng, M.: SLA-aware AI resource allocation for cloud environments. J. Cloud Comput. Adv. Syst. Appl. **8**, 100–113 (2024)
40. Xu, Z., Zhang, R., Yang, C.: IoT-enabled SLA-aware energy optimization in edge systems. IEEE Trans. Green Commun. Netw. **28**(2), 124–138 (2024)
41. Gupta, S., Kumar, V., Mehta, P.: SLA-driven green computing in multi-cloud environments. IEEE Trans. Cloud Comput. **12**(1), 98–110 (2023)

Emerging Applications and Use Cases

Reducing Hip Surgery Time by Automating X-ray Annotations Using Deep Learning

Varsha Bhole, Aditi Amale[✉], Ayushkumar Kamble, and Siddhi Bhatade

Information Technology, A.C. Patil College of Engineering, Kharghar, Maharashtra, India
{vybhole,aditiamale}@acpce.ac.in

Abstract. Hip surgeries require precise and timely interpretation of X-ray images to identify structures, implants, and abnormalities. This research focuses on reducing surgery time by automating the annotation of hip X-rays using deep learning models, specifically YOLOv8 and YOLOv7, which are optimized for object detection in medical imaging. The models accurately identify and label key anatomical features and abnormalities, assisting surgeons with real-time insights that streamline both preoperative planning and intraoperative procedures. By automating annotations, this approach minimizes manual workload, reduces surgery duration, and enhances the precision of surgical interventions, ultimately aiming to improve patient outcomes and surgical efficiency in orthopedic practices.

Keywords: Artificial Intelligence · Deep learning · X- ray annotation · YOLO models · Osteoporosis · Ultralytics

1 Introduction

The demand for orthopedic surgeries, particularly hip surgeries, continues to grow as the aging population and increasing prevalence of musculoskeletal disorders rise. Accurate and timely interpretation of X-ray images is paramount for effective surgical planning and intervention. In hip surgeries, the identification of critical anatomical features, potential abnormalities, and the presence of implants is essential for ensuring optimal outcomes. Traditional methods of annotating X-ray images rely heavily on manual processes, which can be labor-intensive and time-consuming, potentially leading to delays that affect surgical precision. This paper aims to mitigate these challenges by leveraging advanced deep learning techniques to automate the annotation of hip X-rays. Specifically, we utilize two state-of-the-art models, YOLOv8 and YOLOv7, known for their exceptional performance in object detection tasks. These models are designed to provide real-time analysis of hip X-ray images, enabling the rapid identification and labeling of key structures and abnormalities. A significant aspect of this automation is the capability to discern between normal hip conditions and those exhibiting signs of osteoporosis. This differentiation is critical, as the presence of osteoporosis can significantly influence surgical decision-making, including the choice of surgical techniques and the selection of appropriate implants. By integrating automated annotation with the identification of bone conditions, our approach aims to streamline surgical workflows, reduce the manual

© The Author(s), under exclusive license to Springer Nature Switzerland AG 2026
A. K. Somani et al. (Eds.): ICNCS 2025, CCIS 2718, pp. 71–83, 2026.
https://doi.org/10.1007/978-3-032-12544-6_6

effort required by medical professionals, and enhance patient-specific care in orthopedic practice. The implementation of this system is expected to contribute to a reduction in surgery duration and improve overall surgical outcomes. Furthermore, this research seeks to establish a framework for the broader application of deep learning in medical imaging, showcasing its potential to revolutionize the way orthopedic surgeries are conducted. Through this, we aspire to advance the field of orthopedic surgery by providing innovative solutions that align with the ongoing pursuit of efficiency and precision in patient care. The critical need for enhanced efficiency and accuracy in orthopedic surgeries, particularly hip procedures, where timely and precise decision-making is vital for patient outcomes. With the growing prevalence of hip disorders and an aging population, the demand for surgical interventions is on the rise.

2   Dataset Examined

Data cleaning is a crucial step in the data preparation process, ensuring datasets are accurate, consistent, and reliable for analysis. This process involves identifying and rectifying errors, inconsistencies, such as missing values, duplicate entries, formatting issues, and outliers. Typically, the process begins with data profiling and exploratory analysis to assess the data's quality and structure. Techniques such as imputation for missing values, deduplication algorithms for removing duplicates, and data transformation methods for standardizing formats are then applied. Verification checks and quality assurance measures are conducted to ensure the cleaned data adheres to predefined criteria. Effective data cleaning improves data integrity, reduces biases, and enhances the accuracy and reliability of subsequent data analysis and modeling tasks. For this research, the dataset comprised 49 hip X-ray images of both male and female patients, collected from diverse sources such as Kaggle and Roboflow. The data was annotated under the supervision of orthopedic surgeons from Lata Mangeshkar Hospital, Nagpur, using Roboflow, a popular tool for image annotation. During annotation, particular properties were applied consistently to all images.

Auto-Orient ensured that all images were properly oriented, correcting any rotation or flipping issues to maintain uniformity in the dataset. Each image is resized to a standard dimension of 640×640 pixels, preserving aspect ratios while ensuring compatibility with deep learning models. Flipped images horizontally, simulating variations in patient positioning and increasing the model's ability to generalize across different scenarios. A minimum zoom factor of 40% was applied, providing variations in scale and simulating closer views of specific regions of interest within the X-ray images. Images were rotated randomly within a range of −15 to +15 degrees to account for slight misalignments during the original X-ray capture process. The meticulous process of data cleaning and augmentation is particularly vital in medical imaging, where the accuracy and reliability of data directly impact the performance of machine learning models used for diagnosis.

In this paper, data cleaning ensured that all X-ray images were free from distortions, properly oriented, and standardized to a uniform size. This consistency allowed for seamless input into the model, reducing the likelihood of errors caused by data variability. Augmentation techniques like horizontal flipping, zooming, and slight rotations not only increased the dataset size but also simulated real-world variations, such as changes in patient positioning or imaging angles. These enhancements ensured the model's robustness, enabling it to generalize better across unseen data. Overall, this systematic approach laid a solid foundation for developing a reliable and accurate model for detecting abnormalities in hip X-rays, ultimately supporting more effective and timely medical decision-making.

3 Related Work

The research aims to automate the detection of osteoporosis in hip X-rays using advanced object detection models, YOLOv7 and YOLOv8. The dataset consists of annotated hip X-ray images categorized into two groups: normal and osteoporotic bones. These images are sourced from medical databases and hospitals to ensure a diverse range of cases. Each image is carefully annotated, with bounding boxes marking areas of interest, such as bone regions affected by osteoporosis. This labeling process helps in training the models to distinguish between normal and diseased bone structures accurately. Before feeding the data into the models, preprocessing steps are applied to enhance image quality and standardize input dimensions. The X-rays are resized to a consistent format suitable for YOLO models, and pixel values are normalized to improve the detection process. Data augmentation techniques, including rotation, flipping, and scaling, are used to expand the training set's variability. This not only helps in reducing overfitting but also ensures that the model can generalize well across different types of X-ray images. The research utilizes YOLOv7 and YOLOv8 models due to their speed and high accuracy in real-time object detection tasks. Both models are fine-tuned using transfer learning, starting with pretrained weights that are then adjusted to the specific characteristics of the hip X-ray dataset. Hyperparameters such as learning rate, batch size, and number of training epochs are optimized for better performance [1].

3.1 Osteoporosis

Osteoporosis is a silent enemy that may not be felt before bone fragments appear, but when a person is getting older, the bone mass is consistently decreasing in the body. Osteoporosis causes diminution of the brain's bone mineral density and thus makes the bones in the hip, spine, and wrist easily fractured. This is the leading cause of bone metabolism dysfunction. The function of bone is to distribute cells as a living matter [4]. This procedure is kept up by the body which keeps demolishing the old bone cells but simultaneously regenerates it with new cells. These mechanisms are faster during the various stages of life. Inherent in childhood and adolescence, there would be rapid change in the bone synthesis, a consequent larger BMD could be measured, which peaks at about 20. Between the 7th and 10th year, the rate of new bone production is equal to the rate of decomposition of the old bone, and the adult skeleton is fully replaced. Bone mineral density (BMD) naturally begins to decline after the age of 40 due to an imbalance between bone formation and bone breakdown [9, 11]. Although new bone continues to form, the rate of bone loss surpasses the rate of growth, resulting in thinner and more brittle bones. This weakening process primarily affects the outer layer of the bone, making it more prone to fractures [14].

BMD is most commonly measured using a technique called DXA (Dual-Energy X-ray Absorptiometry), which provides a clear assessment of bone health. These measurements are critical for diagnosing osteoporosis, a condition characterized by porous and fragile bones. A lower BMD value indicates a higher likelihood of developing osteoporosis. Another important diagnostic tool is the T-score, which is derived from BMD measurements. The T-score compares a person's BMD to that of a healthy young adult. It is calculated using the formula in Eq. 1:

$$T - score = (BMD - YN)/SD \tag{1}$$

Here, YN represents the expected BMD of a young, healthy individual, and SD is the standard deviation of BMD in young people. According to the World Health Organization (WHO), T-score values are classified as follows T-score > -1: Normal bone density $-1 \leq$ T-score < -2.5: Low bone mass (osteopenia) T-score ≤ -2.5: Osteoporosis. As people age, bone loss accelerates, and monitoring both BMD and T-scores becomes crucial. These indicators help assess bone health and predict the risk of fractures. However, it is essential to note that osteoporosis in the hip specifically requires a clinical diagnosis [1, 4, 10].

3.2 Artificial Intelligence and Deep Learning in Osteoporosis

Deep learning has revolutionized the field of medical imaging, providing powerful tools for object detection and classification. Convolutional Neural Networks (CNNs), a cornerstone of deep learning, have achieved impressive accuracy across various imaging modalities, including X-rays, MRIs, and CT scans [3]. These networks excel in learning hierarchical features from images, making them highly effective for identifying subtle patterns and abnormalities. Advancements in architectures such as YOLO (You Only Look Once) have further propelled real-time object detection in clinical settings. Unlike traditional methods that process images in stages, YOLO processes the entire image in a single step, offering high-speed and precise detection. This capability makes it particularly suitable for clinical applications where time and accuracy are critical [1, 4]. The integration of artificial intelligence (AI) into orthopedic surgery holds immense potential to transform practice. Automated annotation systems powered by AI can streamline workflows by reducing the time required for manual annotations, enabling surgeons to focus on critical tasks. This reduction in surgical duration enhances efficiency and may lead to better patient outcomes. Additionally, AI-driven systems improve the accuracy of preoperative planning by providing precise measurements and identifying key anatomical landmarks, thus aiding in the preparation for complex procedures [2].

An exemplary application of deep learning in orthopedics is HipXNet, developed by Blüthgen et al. (2020), which demonstrated the feasibility of using AI for diagnosing hip osteoarthritis. HipXNet leverages deep learning algorithms to analyze radiographs and identify signs of osteoarthritis with high accuracy, supporting radiologists and orthopedic surgeons in making informed decisions. Furthermore, AI tools are invaluable in medical education and training, offering consistent and objective assessments of radiographic images. These tools help trainees develop their diagnostic skills by providing immediate feedback, enhancing their ability to interpret complex cases. Overall, the integration of deep learning in medical imaging and orthopedic surgery not only enhances diagnostic precision but also paves the way for more efficient and effective clinical workflows [8, 15].

3.3 Convolution Neural Network (CNN) Model

Convolutional Neural Networks (CNNs) are a specialized class of deep learning models designed to process and analyze visual data. They have become the backbone of modern medical imaging applications, including the detection and diagnosis of orthopedic conditions. CNNs are particularly effective due to their ability to automatically learn spatial hierarchies of features from raw images, such as edges, textures, and more complex patterns, without requiring manual feature extraction. This makes them well-suited for analyzing radiological images like X-rays, MRIs, and CT scans. In the context of orthopedic surgery, CNNs have shown remarkable performance in tasks such as identifying fractures, detecting joint displacements, and classifying bone conditions like osteoporosis or osteoarthritis. For example, models like YOLO (which build upon CNN principles) are used to detect specific areas of interest in X-ray images in real-time, allowing for rapid assessment of hip joint abnormalities. CNN-based systems can also precisely locate anatomical landmarks, such as the femoral neck or acetabulum, which are critical for preoperative planning and implant placement [6, 4]. Moreover, CNNs enable automated annotation of medical images by detecting abnormalities and segmenting regions of interest with high accuracy. This reduces the manual effort required from radiologists and surgeons while maintaining consistency in results. By leveraging large annotated datasets, CNNs can continuously improve their performance through training, making them an invaluable tool in clinical workflows [5].

For example, models like HipXNet utilize CNNs to assist in diagnosing hip osteoarthritis, demonstrating how these networks can provide reliable, objective insights to support medical decision-making. In addition to aiding in diagnosis, CNNs are transforming medical education by offering interactive training tools. These tools simulate real-world scenarios, allowing trainees to practice interpreting radiographs and receive feedback based on CNN-generated predictions. This ensures that medical professionals are well-equipped to handle complex cases, ultimately improving patient care in orthopedic settings. The application of CNNs in orthopedic diagnosis has significantly enhanced the speed and accuracy of clinical decision-making [6, 3]. Modern CNN architectures, such as ResNet, Inception, and EfficientNet, have introduced deeper and more efficient layers for learning intricate patterns in medical images [1]. These models are capable of distinguishing between subtle differences in bone density, joint spacing, and structural integrity, which are essential for diagnosing conditions like osteoporosis, fractures, and osteoarthritis. By incorporating advanced techniques such as transfer learning, CNNs can achieve high accuracy even with relatively small datasets, a common challenge in medical imaging. Additionally, the use of CNNs reduces interobserver variability, ensuring consistent diagnoses across different medical practitioners. This reliability not only improves diagnostic confidence but also facilitates early detection of orthopedic issues, enabling timely interventions and better patient outcomes. Through continuous innovation, CNNs are poised to become an integral part of orthopedic diagnostics, offering scalable solutions for both clinical and research applications [3, 5].

4 Proposed Systems

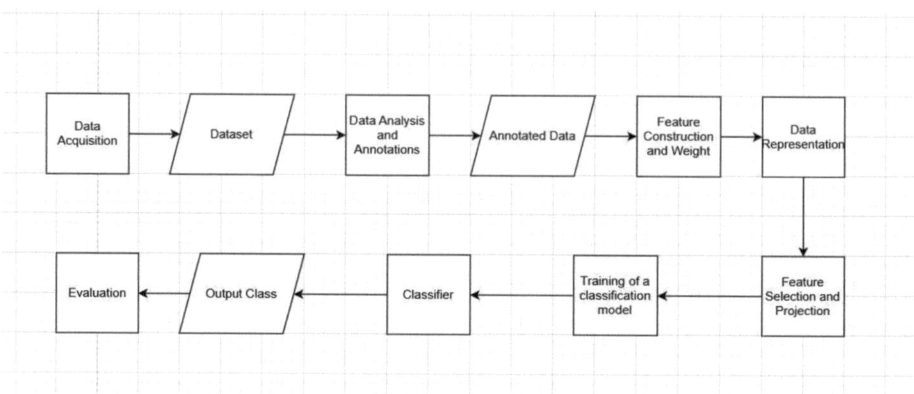

Fig. 1. Sequence Diagram

The architecture is designed to efficiently automate the annotation of hip X-ray images while identifying conditions such as normal bone density and osteoporosis. This section outlines the core components of the system architecture, emphasizing how each module contributes to the overall functionality and performance.

Data Ingestion

The process begins with data ingestion, where hip X-ray images are collected from various sources, including medical databases and clinical settings. These images serve as the raw data for analysis, aimed at detecting abnormalities related to osteoporosis. Each image is transformed into a structured format suitable for processing by the deep learning model. In this stage, the accumulation of diverse data sources, including patient records and clinical guidelines, enriches the knowledge base. This information is then preprocessed to standardize the images, ensuring uniformity in pixel intensity, resolution, and format.

Image Processing

Once the X-ray images are ingested, they undergo several preprocessing steps. These steps include image normalization and resizing, which prepare the images for accurate analysis by the deep learning model. The preprocessing stage is vital as it enhances the quality of input data, enabling the model to focus on relevant anatomical features associated with osteoporosis detection.

Model Training

The preprocessed X-ray images are used to train advanced deep learning architectures, specifically YOLOv8 and YOLOv7. These models are designed for object detection, allowing them to identify and annotate abnormalities associated with osteoporosis, such as fractures or changes in bone structure. The models are initially pre-trained on a wide variety of medical images and then fine-tuned on a specialized dataset focusing on hip X-ray images. This training process is essential for achieving high accuracy in detecting various bone conditions, including normal bone density and osteoporosis.

Classification and Severity Prediction

During the classification phase, the models utilize a SoftMax activation function in the final layer to predict the probabilities of different bone density conditions, including normal bone density, low bone density (osteopenia), and severe osteoporosis. The output generates a probabilistic distribution across these categories, allowing the system to classify the patient's condition based on the analyzed X-ray image. This classification process is critical for providing an accurate assessment of bone health and guiding clinical decision-making.

Output Visualization

The system outputs the classification results, which can be visualized through heatmaps, bounding boxes, or direct labels over the X-ray images, highlighting regions with abnormalities. This visualization aids radiologists and orthopedic surgeons in understanding the extent of the condition and making informed decisions regarding treatment options. Additionally, the system may provide a numerical or categorical assessment of the severity of osteoporosis, such as mild, moderate, or severe osteoporosis.

Evaluation

To ensure the accuracy and reliability of the model, performance metrics are evaluated throughout the training and testing phases. The model is optimized using the Adam optimizer, which dynamically adjusts the learning rate for efficient training. The evaluation primarily focuses on accuracy, measuring the percentage of correctly classified images and ensuring that the system meets the clinical standards required for effective patient care.

5   Result and Discussion

In this study, we developed a deep learning model aimed at automating the annotation of hip X-rays to assist in reducing surgery time. The model was trained to detect and classify bone health conditions, such as "normal" and "osteoporotic" states, to provide rapid, accurate diagnoses that inform surgical planning.

5.1   Model Accuracy and Classification Effectiveness

The initial results from our model's evaluation, shown in Fig. 1, highlight the classification accuracy for hip health detection. The deep learning model achieved an accuracy of 0.62 for identifying osteoporotic hips and 0.59 for normal hips on the provided X-ray images. These probabilities reflect the model's confidence in classification, indicating a promising level of precision suitable for clinical application. The distinction between normal and osteoporotic hips is crucial in orthopedic surgery, as the bone condition informs the approach and potential risk mitigation strategies. This automated annotation can enhance pre-operative planning by providing surgeons with immediate insights, potentially reducing decision-making time during surgery.

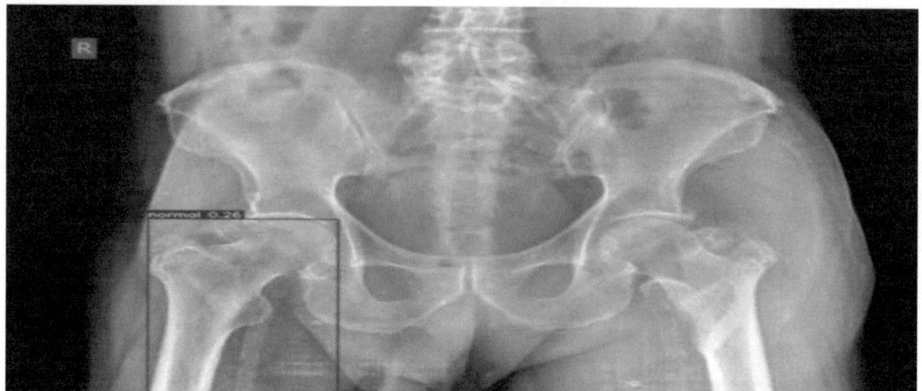

Fig. 2. X-ray Image with Model Annotations

5.2 YOLOv7

YOLOv7 (You Only Look Once version 7) is a state-of-the-art deep learning model designed for real-time object detection tasks, making it highly suitable for applications in medical imaging and orthopedic diagnosis. As an improvement over its predecessors, YOLOv7 offers enhanced accuracy and faster inference times, making it ideal for processing X-ray images in clinical environments. This model excels at detecting and classifying objects within images, such as fractures, joint abnormalities, or osteoporotic changes in bone structure, with minimal processing delay. YOLOv7's architecture efficiently handles large datasets of medical images, which is crucial for tasks like hip joint evaluation or the detection of bone conditions such as arthritis or osteoporosis. Its ability to detect and localize multiple abnormalities in a single pass makes it a valuable tool for orthopedic surgeons, enabling rapid assessment and more accurate preoperative planning. Moreover, YOLOv7's robustness in real-time processing allows it to be integrated into clinical workflows, offering automated annotation and analysis to assist healthcare professionals in diagnosing and monitoring orthopedic conditions.

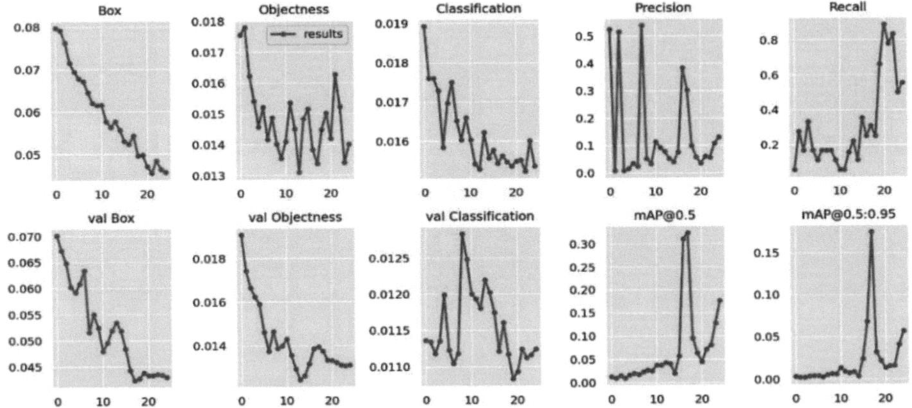

Fig. 3. Graphs for box loss, objectness loss, classification loss, precision, recall and mean average precision (mAP@0.5 & mAP@0.95) over training and validation sets on YOLO v7

Table 1. Precision, Recall, And Mean Average Precision Values of YOLOv7 on Hip X-Ray Dataset

Classes	Evaluation Metrics			
	Precision	Recall	mAP@0.5	mAP@0.5:0.95
All Classes	0.820	0.788	0.909	0.822
Normal	0.939	0.700	0.908	0.849
Osteoporotic	0.700	0.875	0.910	0.795

5.3 YOLOv8

YOLOv8 (You Only Look Once version 8) is the latest iteration of the YOLO series, offering cutting-edge advancements in real-time object detection, and is becoming increasingly relevant for medical imaging, particularly in orthopedic applications. YOLOv8 builds upon the strengths of previous versions, with a more refined architecture that enhances both accuracy and speed. In the context of orthopedic imaging, YOLOv8 is highly effective for tasks such as detecting fractures, joint displacements, and other skeletal abnormalities from X-ray or MRI scans. It offers significant improvements in precision and detection of smaller and more complex features, making it a powerful tool for analyzing the fine details of bone structures.

One of the key advantages of YOLOv8 in orthopedic applications is its ability to perform real-time object detection while maintaining high accuracy. This allows for quick analysis of X-ray images, reducing the time it takes for radiologists and surgeons to assess and make decisions. YOLOv8's improved feature extraction capabilities allow it to detect multiple conditions within a single image, such as joint misalignment, fractures, and the early stages of osteoporotic bone loss. Moreover, YOLOv8's design is optimized for running on various hardware platforms, from high-performance servers to edge devices, making it adaptable to different clinical environments.

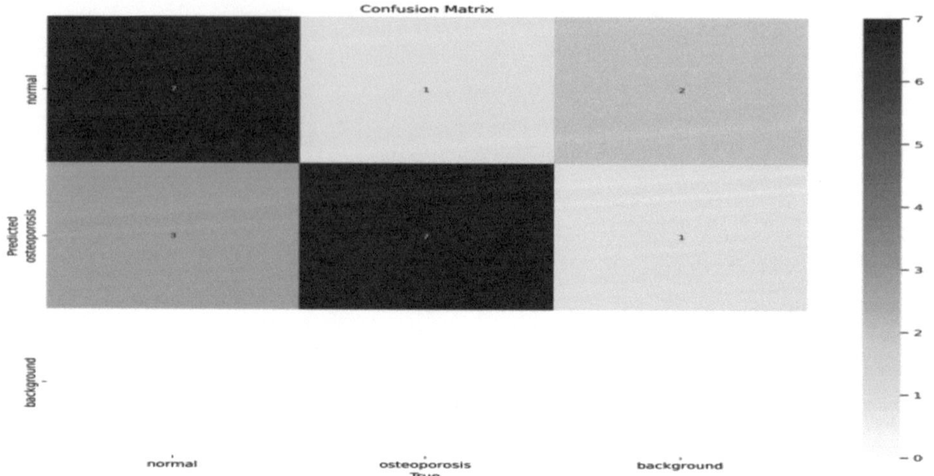

Fig. 4. Confusion matrix for X-Ray data of hips two classes: a) Normal, and b) Osteoporosis, along with an additional background class trained on the YOLO v8 mod

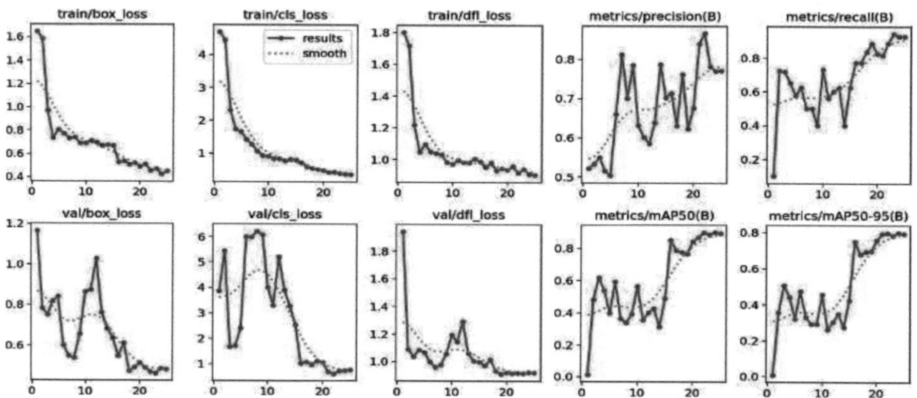

Fig. 5. Graphs for box loss, objectness loss, classification loss, precision, recall and mean average precision (mAP@0.5 & mAP@0.95) over training and validation sets on YOLO v8

Table 2. Precision, Recall, And Mean Average Precision Values Of Yolov8 Ultralytics On Hip X-Ray Dataset

Classes	Evaluation Metrics			
	Precision	Recall	mAP@0.5	mAP@0.5:0.95
All Classes	0.929	0.904	0.988	0.888
Normal	1.000	0.807	0.995	0.889
Osteoporotic	0.858	1.000	0.982	0.887

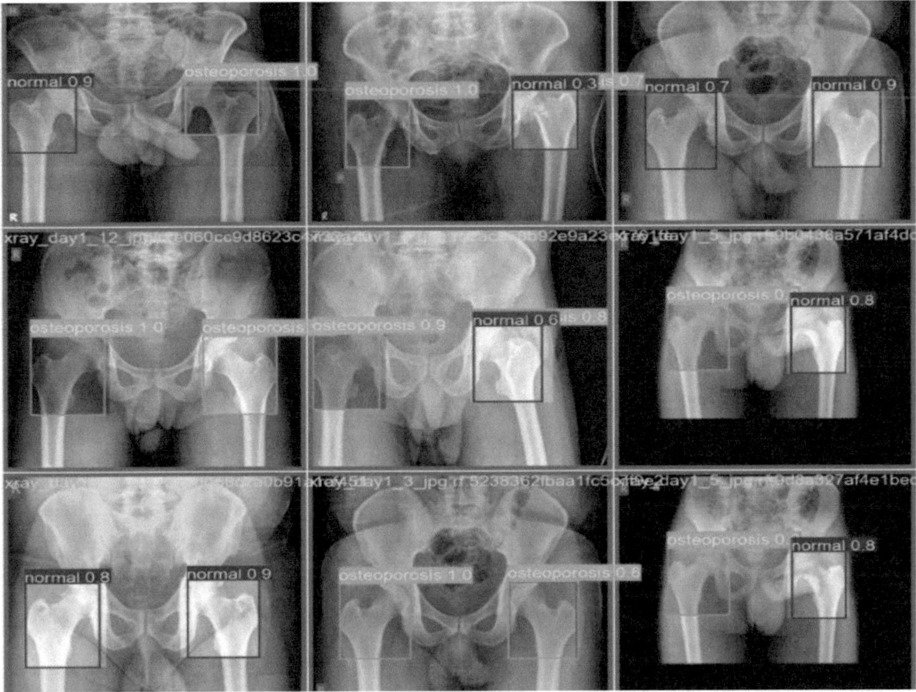

Fig. 6. Ultralytics YOLOv8 prediction results on the validation set of hip X-Ray dataset labeling the confidence on the bone being predicted as normal or osteoporotic.

6 Conclusion and Future Work

Osteoporosis, a bone disease, is mainly caused by lower bone mass and greater risk of fracture. The DEXA image-based bone mineral density (BMD) scan is a cutting-edge innovative technique for early diagnosis of and accurate treatment for osteoporosis, which has turned out to be the gold standard method of dependable osteoporosis discovery. Nevertheless, the downfall of the method is that it's not shelf- advantageous and people who are below the poverty line cannot afford it. Hence, this is the reason why the report asserts using deep learning methods on X-Ray film in place of DEXA by implementing this research. Dependent on the X-Ray image set of hips basically consisting of 117 images obtained later, the article presents and compares deep literacy algorithms employed for the same task YOLOv7, and Ultralytics YOLO v8 models. Out of the four algorithms accounted for, the YOLO v8 model exhibited the highest sensitivity in the conducted study. Several paramount factors, which are key to the YOLO v8 endoskeleton, are credited with this unusually good performance. At first, the YOLO (You Only Look formerly) database group prides itself on real- time object discovery efficiency. YOLO v8, specifically, uses a simple composite neural network armature that predicts the bounding boxes and the chances of the class directly on a condensed lattice, which, in turn, provides faster termination times than other objects detection models. Furthermore, YOLO v8 has an abundance of architectural improvements and is technologically superior to its predecessors, such as the integration of point aggregation networks, anchor- ground predictions, and point-unwinding.

Future improvements include extending the model to 3D imaging modalities like CT and MRI for better anatomical insight. Real-time surgeon feedback and personalization features can enhance model accuracy and user adaptability. Training on diverse datasets and using federated learning can improve generalization while maintaining data privacy. Further developments may involve automated abnormality detection, integration with AR for intraoperative guidance, and alignment with clinical regulations. Combining imaging data with patient records could offer predictive analytics, and future integration with robotic surgery systems could support precise surgical planning and execution.

Declaration

The authors declare that they have not used any type of generative artificial intelligence for the writing of this manuscript, nor for the creation of images, graphics, tables, or their corresponding captions.

References

1. Kawade, V., Naikwade, V.: A comparative analysis of deep learning models and conventional approaches for osteoporosis detection in hip X-Ray images. In: IEEE Explore (2023). https://doi.org/10.1109/WCONF58270.2023.10235129
2. Fraiwan, M., Al-Kofahi, N., Ibnian, A., Hanatleh, O.: Detection of developmental dysplasia of the hip in X-ray images using deep transfer learning. BMC Med. Inf. Decis. Making **22**(1), 216 (2022). https://doi.org/10.1186/s12911-022-01957-9
3. Zhang, Y., Ding, X., Qin, H., Liang, X., Liang, R.: Automated detection of hip fracture in radiographs based on convolutional neural networks. In: 2022 IEEE International Conference on Mechatronics and Automation (ICMA) (pp. 2565–2570). IEEE (2022). https://doi.org/10.1109/ICMA52036.2022.9816370
4. Blüthgen, C., et al.: HipXNet: radiological diagnosis of hip osteoarthritis using deep convolutional neural networks. Eur. J. Radiol. **132**, 109272 (2020). https://doi.org/10.1016/j.ejrad.2020.109272
5. Yang, X., Lian, C., Zheng, Y., Zhang, M., Yang, X., Li, S.: A two-stage framework for hip fracture diagnosis and surgery assistance in X-Ray images using deep neural networks. Appl. Sci. **14**(1), 133 (2024). https://doi.org/10.3390/app14010133
6. Balanika, S.T., Vrizidou, S., Drosos, C., Baltas, C.: Radiographic interpretation of hip replacement hardware. A pictorial essay. In: Proc. Eur. Congr. Radiol. (ESSR) (2014). https://doi.org/10.1594/essr2014/P-0050
7. Szegedy, C., Vanhoucke, V., Ioffe, S., Shlens, J., Wojna, Z.: Rethinking the inception architecture for computer vision. In: Proceedings of IEEE Conf. Comput. Vis. Pattern Recognit. (CVPR), Las Vegas, NV, USA, pp. 2818–2826 (2016). https://doi.org/10.1109/CVPR.2016.308
8. Xu, W., et al.: A deep-learning aided diagnostic system in assessing developmental dysplasia of the hip on pediatric pelvic radiographs. In: Frontiers in Pediatrics, vol. 9 (2021). https://doi.org/10.3389/fped.2021.785480
9. Faulkner, K.G.: The tale of the T-score: review and perspective. Osteoporos. Int. **16**, 347–352 (2004). [CrossRef]
10. Cosman, F., et al.: Clinician's guide to prevention and treatment of osteoporosis. Osteoporos. Int. **25**, 2359–2381 (2014). [CrossRef]

11. Hung, S.-K., Hsu, W.-Y., Shih, H.-Y., Lin, H.-C., Hu, Y.-H.: Combination hip X-ray image features extraction and machine learning predictive osteopenia and osteoporosis. Taiwan Soc. Radiol. Technol. **40**, 59–67 (2016)
12. Yoo, T.K., et al.: Osteoporosis risk prediction for bone mineral density assessment of postmenopausal women using machine learning. Yonsei Med. J. **54**, 1321–1330 (2013). [CrossRef]
13. Adams, J.W., Zhang, Z., Noetscher, G.M., Nazarian, A., Makarov, S.N.: Application of a neural network classifier to radiofrequency-based osteopenia/osteoporosis screening. IEEE J. Transl. Eng. Health Med. **9**, 4900907 (2021). [CrossRef]
14. Ribeiro, M., Monteiro, F.J., Ferraz, M.P.: Infection of orthopedic implants with emphasis on bacterial adhesion process and techniques used in studying bacterial-material interactions. Biomatter **2**(4), 176194 (2012)
15. Ching, H.A., Choudhury, D., Nine, M.J., Osman, N.A.A.: Effects of surface coating on reducing friction and wear of orthopaedic implants. Sci. Technol. Adv. Mater. **15**(1), 014402 (2014)
16. Feng, S.-W., Lin, S.-Y., Chiang, Y.-H., Lu, M.-H., Chao, Y.-H.: Deep learning-based hip X-ray image analysis for predicting osteoporosis. In: Applied Sciences, vol. 14 (2024). https://doi.org/10.3390/app14010133

Depression Detection Among College Students Using Social Network

Pratiksha Deshmukh[(✉)] [iD] and Harshali Patil [iD]

Thakur College of Engineering and Technology, Mumbai, Maharashtra, India
{pratiksha.deshmukh,harshali.patil}@tcetmumbai.in

Abstract. Compared to preceding decades, depression is now more common at an earlier stage of life. Because of the demands to become independent and create a distinct identity, adolescence, a crucial developmental stage marked by the passage from infancy to adulthood, often results in emotional instability. According to research, treating child depression quickly may have considerable long-term advantages and lead to better overall results for the children's mental health. Adolescents have a better chance of enjoying favourable long-term outcomes and a higher quality of life if they can identify and treat depressive symptoms early. This research study's primary goal was to evaluate and analyse the many variables that affect college students in India who experience depression. Using a cross-sectional study approach, the essential data was gathered. An online survey on Google was used to gather the data, and a total of 405 people responded to it. It is essential for educational institutions to provide instruction on this mental health issue to college students to increase their ability to recognise and comprehend depression. Colleges may provide students with the skills they need to accurately recognise and diagnose depression's symptoms by providing them with thorough information and understanding about the condition.

Keywords: Depression · Mental Health · Social Networks · Students · SPSS

1 Introduction

The definition of depression strongly emphasizes its syndrome and medical components. Similar to disorders seen in other medical specialties, it denotes a collection of signs and symptoms that commonly co-occur and are thought to result from a single underlying cause (Paykel, 2022). Even though the precise pathophysiology may not be understood, it is believed to vary depending on the situation and may have unique underlying causes. A wide variety of emotional lows, from a modest sense of melancholy to the intense and upsetting thoughts of suicide, are included in depression. It is a typical mental health disorder brought on by the difficulties and strains of daily living (Firth-Cozens, 2023). People who are depressed or unhappy usually restore emotional stability within a fair amount of time. However, there are times when these grievous or unhappy sensations last for a long time and become more significant than the original reason. Consequently, the afflicted person could stop engaging in their usual social, professional, and personal

A. K. Somani et al. (Eds.): ICNCS 2025, CCIS 2718, pp. 84–104, 2026.
https://doi.org/10.1007/978-3-032-12544-6_7

pursuits. In such circumstances, it is essential to take the likelihood of a depression diagnosis into account and to seek the proper support and assistance (Kraus et al., 2019). There could be several factors affecting the chances of an individual getting depression. With its rapid access to information and ease of connection, the Internet has unquestionably improved our lives. However, it's crucial to recognize that the Internet may also inspire undesirable behaviors for a sizable portion of people. Ivan Goldberg, a psychologist, first used the term "Internet Addiction" (IA) to describe pathological, compulsive internet use (Bisen and Deshpande, 2020). On the other hand, Ostracism, also known as social exclusion, may negatively affect a person's mental health and social and psychological functioning. Additionally, social isolation could possibly be a significant factor in the development and persistence of mental illnesses. Fundamental human needs like fulfilment, belongingness, self-esteem, control, and a feeling of purpose in life are undermined by these experiences. People's basic needs are frustrated when they are socially isolated, which may harm their general mental health and quality of life (Seidl et al., 2020). This paper aims to investigate the elements that influence depression among Indian college students. The paper will also examine the crucial elements that affect college students' mental health, paying particular attention to the elements that are pertinent to depression. Additionally, this study will identify these factors and provide helpful advice for reducing or resolving the depression problem among Indian college students. In this research, the aim, objective, and hypothesis are taken into consideration is given below.

1.1 Aim

The aim of the topic is to determine the main factors that influence depression of college students in India.

1.2 Objectives

1. To investigate the influence of Perceived usefulness on Depression of college students
2. To determine the impact of Perceived ease of use on Depression of college students
3. To identify the influence of Perceived enjoyment of use on behavioral intention of college students
4. To investigate the influence of Social influence of use on Depression of college students
5. To determine the major factors (Behavioral Intention, Anxiety, Preferred Social Media and Internet Experience) influence Depression of college students.

1.3 Hypothesis

H1: Perceived usefulness (PU) has a positive influence on users' Depression to regularly use their preferred social media platform.

H2: Perceived ease of use (PEoU) has a positive influence on users' Depression to frequently use social networks.

H3: Perceived enjoyment (EN) has a positive influence on users' Depression to continue using social networks for communication.

H4: Social influence (SI) has a positive influence on users' Depression to use social networks as recommended or encouraged by friends and family.

H5: Trust (TR) has a positive influence on users' Depression to trust the accuracy and reliability of information shared on social networks.

2 Literature Review

Anxiety and Changes in Conduct: Social media now has a more significant and more substantial influence on people's lives than any other medium, outpacing it in both scope and size (Patil, H. P., & Atique, M. 2015, Patil, H.P. & Atique, M. 2020). Although social networking sites were initially intended to promote connection and improve well-being generally, recent research indicates that excessive use of social media may actually have adverse effects, including feelings of loneliness, increased anxiety, and a higher risk of developing depression (Goel and Gupta, 2020). People with social anxiety disorder may shy away from or act reservedly in social settings. Having an extensive network of friends on social media platforms may contribute to developing this illness by making one envious of their ideal life and online relationships. The development of social anxiety is also influenced by one's beliefs of how others see them, whether those perceptions are accurate or not. It is important to remember that students who use social media excessively lose productivity and have numerous physical and mental health issues, such as elevated stress levels, anxiety, and panic (Jiang and Ngien, 2020). Social media platforms could be examples of the influence of perceived usefulness as a person's perception of how technologies, or a specific technology, are purposely designed to better their jobs or responsibilities in a way that promotes efficiency and effectiveness is referred to as perceived usefulness (Bolodeoku et al., 2022). On the other hand, the term "perceived ease of use" (PEOU) describes how convinced or confident people are that a specific system, such as online shopping, is straightforward. A system is more likely to be welcomed and adopted by users if seen as simple (Ferdianto, 2022). For example, numerous youngsters in India who are in school or getting ready for college exhibit various behavioral abnormalities due to inadequate physical exercise. In addition to encouraging a sedentary lifestyle, these changes also make young people feel anxious and helpless. Their mental and emotional health has suffered due to their lack of physical exercise in various ways (News18, 2021). This could be a result of Anxiety and Changes in Conduct.

FOMO and Mental Illness: The use of social media and the FOMO (fear of missing out) problem are closely related, especially among teens. The constant worry about missing out on enjoyable events that others could be experiencing is known as FOMO. Because of this concern, they find it difficult to focus and have a solid want to follow other people's activity on social media platforms all the time (Fabris et al., 2020). This could be mentioned as an example of Social influence, which refers to various intentional and unintentional techniques that affect people's attitudes, beliefs, or behaviors. It differs from the purposeful and prepared act of persuasion, which often requires the target's knowledge in that it may happen accidentally or indirectly (Singh, Sinha and Liébana-Cabanillas, 2020). For example, a family member of an 18-year-old boy brought him to the Central Institute of Psychiatry (CIP) in Kanke, Ranchi. They reported that he hadn't gone to college for the previous two months, that he was terrified to leave the home, and that he hadn't eaten or drunk anything for the previous four to five days (The Economic Times, 2022).

Cyberbullying: Bullying is sometimes defined as a pattern of persistently violent behavior that is characterized by an unbalanced power dynamic between the victim and the offender. It involves displaying angry behavior repeatedly and continuously for a long time. Cyberbullying, a key expression of this epidemic that has arisen in the age of technology, differs from conventional bullying in that it primarily takes place on different social media platforms and other online places. Young people are more susceptible to cyberbullying, which has raised a lot of social anxiety. Derogatory and harsh language is often used in cyberbullying, which worsens the effects on the victims (Cheng et al., 2019). Cyberbullying could also result in increasing stress and anxiety in the victims. According to a recent poll by Minhas (2023a) in India, in May 2022, a sizable percentage of people between the ages of 24 and 34 have reported feeling more anxious and concerned lately. Comparatively, the research discovered that 28% of individuals between the ages of 16 and 24 experienced constant levels of stress and worry.

3   Research Method

The research was quantitative in nature, along with deductive research methodology being used in this study, where the conclusions were inferred from existing theories and concepts. The study followed the tenets of positivism, a philosophical viewpoint that emphasises using empirical evidence and scientific methods to learn new things. A descriptive method was used to describe the study design to explain the research issue clearly. For primary data collection, Google surveys were used to collect replies from a total of 405 people to acquire primary data, guaranteeing the accuracy and legitimacy of the data gathered.

4   Data Analysis Technique

Numerous statistical tests were used on the data to analyse it appropriately. Key tests such as the independent T-test, correlation, and regression testing were used in addition to the frequency and descriptive tests. The main goal of using these tests was to fully comprehend the data and reveal any noteworthy correlations or patterns that could be present. Researchers sought to extensively examine the data, revealing significant connections and spotting remarkable patterns by combining these tests.

5   Finding and Analysis

5.1   Frequency Test

The data from the survey comprises replies from 405 respondents, as shown in Table 1. Out of 405 respondents, 37% of them identified as male, 59% as female, and 4% said they would rather not say, as shown in Fig. 1. Females made up the bulk of the responders.

Table 1. Gender

Gender	Frequency	Percent	Cumulative Percent
Male	150	37	37
Female	239	59	96
Prefer Not to Say	16	4	100
Total	405	100	

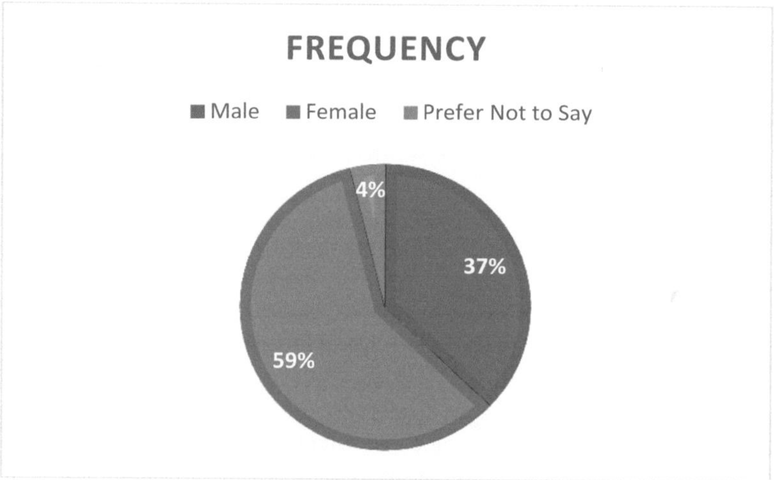

Fig. 1. Frequency Analysis based on Gender Factor

Table 2. Age Factor

Age	Frequency	Percent	Cumulative Percent
18–25 years	209	51.6	51.6
26–30 years	136	33.6	85.2
More than 35 years	60	14.8	100
Total	405	100	

Table 2 shows that 51.6% of the 405 survey respondents were between the ages of 18 and 25; 33.6% were between the ages of 26 and 30, and 14.8% were 35 or older. The age range of 18 to 25 was represented by most responders, followed by 26 to 30 (Figs. 2 and 3).

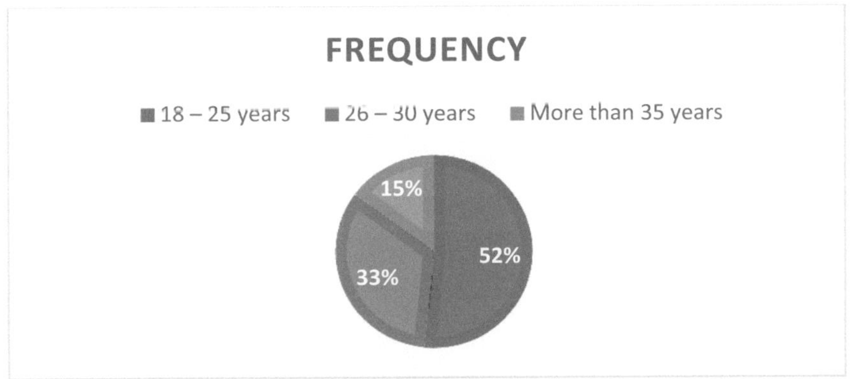

Fig. 2. Frequency Analysis based on Age Factor

Table 3. Education Level

		Frequency	Percent	Cumulative Percent
Valid	**High School Diploma/GED**	127	31.4	31.4
	Associate's Degree	158	39.0	70.4
	Bachelor's Degree	91	22.5	92.8
	Master's Degree	29	7.2	100.0
	Total	405	100.0	

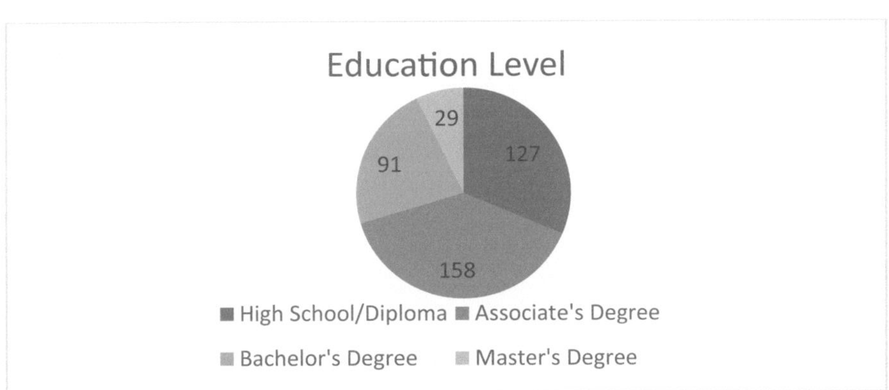

Fig. 3. Frequency Analysis based on Education Level

5.2 Reliability Test

An extraordinarily high degree of internal consistency and reliability among the 35 test items is shown by the Cronbach's Alpha result of 0.995. This implies that the items are valid for evaluating the target variable and measuring the same underlying concept (Tables 3 and 4).

Table 4. Reliability Test

Cronbach's Alpha	No. of Items
0.995	35

5.3 Descriptive Test

With a mean score of 2.38 and a standard deviation of 1.562, the data shows that respondents believe social networks are helpful for keeping in touch with friends and family. However, it is noteworthy that social networks may enhance communication, as stated by every responder, yielding a mean score of 1.00 with no standard deviation. With a mean score of 2.38 and a standard deviation of 1.417, the data also shows that respondents believe social networks are helpful for maintaining relationships. With a mean score of 2.81 and a standard deviation of 1.422, the behavioral intention to utilize social networks shows a range of answers. For certain variables, the data displays a pattern that is somewhat negatively skewed, pointing to departures from complete normalcy (Table 5).

Table 5. Descriptive Statistics of H1

	N	Minimum	Maximum	Mean	Std. Deviation	Skewness		Kurtosis	
	Statistic	Statistic	Statistic	Statistic	Statistic	Statistic	Std. Error	Statistic	Std. Error
social networks for staying connected with friends and family (Perceived Usefulness)	405	1	5	2.38	1.562	0.64	0.121	−1.214	0.242
social networks can help improve your communication (Perceived Usefulness)	405	1	1	1	0				
social networks to stay connected (Perceived Usefulness)	405	1	5	2.38	1.417	0.591	0.121	−1.02	0.242
symptoms of depression (Depression)	405	1	2	1.74	0.44	−1.088	0.121	−0.82	0.242

(continued)

Table 5. (*continued*)

	N	Minimum	Maximum	Mean	Std. Deviation	Skewness		Kurtosis	
	Statistic	Statistic	Statistic	Statistic	Statistic	Statistic	Std. Error	Statistic	Std. Error
using social networks has a positive impact on your mood and reduces depressive feelings (Depression)	405	1	5	3.25	1.51	−0.23	0.121	−1.423	0.242
experience a decrease in depressive symptoms due to using social networks (Depression)	405	1	5	3.41	1.486	−0.326	0.121	−1.436	0.242

With a mean score of 2.02 and a standard deviation of 1.363, the data shows that users generally regard using social networks and navigating through them to be reasonably straightforward. With a mean score of 2.20 and a standard deviation of 1.338, users also said that they were generally at ease using social media. With a mean score of 2.51 and a standard deviation of 1.417, people also believe that the convenience of utilizing social networks increases their desire to use them often. For certain factors, the data display patterns that are somewhat positively skewed, deviating from complete normalcy (Table 6).

Table 6. Descriptive Statistics of H2

	N	Minimum	Maximum	Mean	Std. Deviation	Skewness		Kurtosis	
	Statistic	Statistic	Statistic	Statistic	Statistic	Statistic	Std. Error	Statistic	Std. Error
navigate and use social networks (Perceived Ease of Use)	405	1	5	2.02	1.363	1.103	0.121	−0.194	0.242
feel comfortable using social networks (Perceived Ease of Use)	405	1	5	2.2	1.338	0.797	0.121	−0.756	0.242

(*continued*)

Table 6. (*continued*)

	N	Minimum	Maximum	Mean	Std. Deviation	Skewness		Kurtosis	
	Statistic	Statistic	Statistic	Statistic	Statistic	Statistic	Std. Error	Statistic	Std. Error
social networks regularly based on their ease of use (Perceived Ease of Use)	405	1	5	2.51	1.417	0.373	0.121	−1.315	0.242
symptoms of depression (Depression)	405	1	2	1.74	0.44	−1.088	0.121	−0.82	0.242
using social networks has a positive impact on your mood and reduces depressive feelings (Depression)	405	1	5	3.25	1.51	−0.23	0.121	−1.423	0.242
experience a decrease in depressive symptoms due to using social networks (Depression)	405	1	5	3.41	1.486	−0.326	0.121	−1.436	0.242

With a mean score of 2.81 and a standard deviation of 1.422, the data shows users' modest propensity to interact with others through social networks. The same mean score and standard deviation are reported by users for their desire to utilize social networks for communication in the future. Additionally, users' intentions to frequently utilize social networks are rather strong, with a mean score of 3.18 and a standard deviation of 1.575. Users regard utilizing social networks to be fun, as shown by a mean score of 2.60 and a standard deviation of 1.412. The data exhibit patterns that are somewhat out of whack with perfect normalcy and are slightly favorably biased. Users regard utilizing social networks to be fun, as shown by a mean score of 2.60 and a standard deviation of 1.412. The data exhibit patterns that are somewhat out of whack with perfect normalcy and are slightly favourably biased (Table 7).

Table 7. Descriptive Statistics of H3

	N	Minimum	Maximum	Mean	Std. Deviation	Skewness		Kurtosis	
	Statistic	Statistic	Statistic	Statistic	Statistic	Statistic	Std. Error	Statistic	Std. Error
symptoms of depression (Depression)	405	1	2	1.74	0.44	−1.088	0.121	−0.82	0.242
using social networks has a positive impact on your mood and reduces depressive feelings (Depression)	405	1	5	3.25	1.51	−0.23	0.121	−1.423	0.242
experience a decrease in depressive symptoms due to using social networks (Depression)	405	1	5	3.41	1.486	−0.326	0.121	−1.436	0.242
use social networks enjoyable (Perceived Enjoyment)	405	1	5	2.6	1.412	0.441	0.121	−1.171	0.242
social networks fun and engaging experience (Perceived Enjoyment)	405	1	5	2.31	1.365	0.65	0.121	−0.942	0.242
continue using social networks (Perceived Enjoyment)	405	1	5	2.25	1.13	0.667	0.121	−0.512	0.242

A mean score of 2.81 and a standard deviation of 1.422 indicate that individuals' intentions to interact with others through social networks are modest. Users also indicate a comparable mean score and standard deviation for their future desire to communicate through social networks. Additionally, users' intentions to frequently utilize social networks are rather strong, with a mean score of 3.18 and a standard deviation of 1.575. With a mean score of 2.37 and a standard deviation of 1.404, users are moderately encouraged to utilize social networks in terms of social influence. The usage of social networks by others has a modest impact on users as well, with a mean score of 3.00 and a standard deviation of 1.556. With a mean score of 3.21 and a standard deviation of 1.477, users indicate a stronger inclination to utilize social networks as a result of the influence of others. The data exhibits patterns that are somewhat out of whack with perfect normalcy, showing some departures from that normality (Table 8).

Table 8. Descriptive Statistics of H4

	N	Minimum	Maximum	Mean	Std. Deviation	Skewness		Kurtosis	
	Statistic	Statistic	Statistic	Statistic	Statistic	Statistic	Std. Error	Statistic	Std. Error
symptoms of depression (Depression)	405	1	2	1.74	0.44	−1.088	0.121	−0.82	0.242
using social networks has a positive impact on your mood and reduces depressive feelings (Depression)	405	1	5	3.25	1.51	−0.23	0.121	−1.423	0.242
experience a decrease in depressive symptoms due to using social networks (Depression)	405	1	5	3.41	1.486	−0.326	0.121	−1.436	0.242
encourage to use social networks (Social Influence)	405	1	5	2.37	1.404	0.621	0.121	−1.029	0.242
influenced by others' use of social networks (Social Influence)	405	1	5	3	1.556	−0.064	0.121	−1.563	0.242
use social networks because of the influence of others (Social Influence)	405	1	5	3.21	1.477	−0.171	0.121	−1.381	0.242

A mean score of 2.81 and a standard deviation of 1.422 indicate that individuals' intentions to interact with others through social networks are modest. Similar mean scores and standard deviations are reported by users for their desire to utilize social networks for communication in the future. Users also indicate a greater likelihood of routinely using social networks, with a mean score of 3.18 and a standard deviation of 1.575. With a mean score of 3.40 and a standard deviation of 1.505, consumers' confidence in social networks to secure their personal information is generally strong. With a mean score of 3.71 and a standard deviation of 1.479, users also exhibit a greater degree of confidence in the veracity and dependability of material published on social networks. Due to their moderate confidence in social networks, users exhibit a moderate inclination to utilize them, as indicated by a mean score of 3.25 and a standard deviation of 1.650. The data exhibits patterns that are somewhat out of whack with perfect normalcy, showing some departures from that normality (Table 9).

Table 9. Descriptive Statistics of H5

	N	Minimum	Maximum	Mean	Std. Deviation	Skewness		Kurtosis	
	Statistic	Statistic	Statistic	Statistic	Statistic	Statistic	Std. Error	Statistic	Std. Error
symptoms of depression (Depression)	405	1	2	1.74	0.44	−1.088	0.121	−0.82	0.242
using social networks has a positive impact on your mood and reduces depressive feelings (Depression)	405	1	5	3.25	1.51	−0.23	0.121	−1.423	0.242
experience a decrease in depressive symptoms due to using social networks (Depression)	405	1	5	3.41	1.486	−0.326	0.121	−1.436	0.242
trust social networks to protect your personal information (Trust)	405	1	5	3.4	1.505	−0.264	0.121	−1.51	0.242

(*continued*)

Table 9. (*continued*)

	N	Minimum	Maximum	Mean	Std. Deviation	Skewness		Kurtosis	
	Statistic	Statistic	Statistic	Statistic	Statistic	Statistic	Std. Error	Statistic	Std. Error
content shared on social networks is accurate and reliable (Trust)	405	1	5	3.71	1.479	−0.753	0.121	−0.949	0.242
use social networks because of the trust (Trust)	405	1	5	3.25	1.65	−0.16	0.121	−1.582	0.242

5.4 Hypothesis Test

All of the variables measuring perceived utility, usability, pleasure, social impact, and trust in social networks had very low (near 0) p-values, showing that the variances between the groups are substantially different. To determine if the mean differences between groups are statistically significant, the "t-test for Equality of Means" offers t-values, degrees of freedom (df), and related p-values. The p-values are similarly very small (around 0) for all variables, showing that the mean differences are statistically significant. The average difference between the groups for each variable is shown by the mean differences. For "Perceived Usefulness," for instance, the mean difference between groups with equal variances assumed and those with unequal variances assumed is − 3.488. This shows that there is a considerable variation in how beneficial the groups are considered by the users, with one group's assessments of usefulness being on average 3.488 units lower than the other. All five hypotheses (H1, H2, H3, H4, and H5) contend that users' depression to use social networks is positively influenced by their respective independent variables (perceived usefulness, perceived ease of use, perceived enjoyment, social influence, and trust). As a result, all theories are chosen (Table 10).

Table 10. Hypothesis Test

		Levene's Test for Equality of Variances		t-test for Equality of Means							
		F	Sig	t	df	Sig. (2-tailed)	Mean Difference	Std. Error Difference	95% Confidence Interval of the Difference		
									Lower	Upper
social networks for staying connected with friends and family (Perceived Usefulness)	Equal variances assumed	1057.261	0	−73.666	281	0	−3.488	0.047	−3.582	−3.395
	Equal variances not assumed	-	-	−67.399	128	0	−3.488	0.052	−3.591	−3.386
navigate and use social networks (Perceived Ease of Use)	Equal variances assumed	426.742	0	−31.695	281	0	−2.736	0.086	−2.906	−2.566
	Equal variances not assumed	-	-	−28.998	128	0	−2.736	0.094	−2.923	−2.55
use social networks enjoyable (Perceived Enjoyment)	Equal variances assumed	32.369	0	−54.199	281	0	−3.159	0.058	−3.274	−3.044
	Equal variances not assumed	-	-	−53.232	246.077	0	−3.159	0.059	−3.276	−3.042
encourage to use social networks (Social Influence)	Equal variances assumed	256.026	0	−60.355	281	0	−3.196	0.053	−3.301	−3.092
	Equal variances not assumed	-	-	−55.517	134.649	0	−3.196	0.058	−3.31	−3.082

(continued)

Table 10. *(continued)*

		Levene's Test for Equality of Variances		t-test for Equality of Means						95% Confidence Interval of the Difference	
		F	Sig	t	df	Sig. (2-tailed)	Mean Difference	Std. Error Difference		Lower	Upper
trust social networks to protect your personal information (Trust)	Equal variances assumed	995.337	0	−80.107	281	0	−3.331	0.042		−3.413	−3.249
	Equal variances not assumed	-	-	−87.551	153	0	−3.331	0.038		−3.406	−3.256

5.5 Regression Analysis

See Tables Table 11, 12 and 13.

Table 11. Model Summary

Model	R	R Square	Adjusted R Square	Std. Error of the Estimate
1	0.973[a]	0.947	0.946	0.402

a. Predictors include: using social networks to stay in touch with friends and family (Perceived Usefulness), believing that social networks will protect your personal information (Trust), finding it easy to navigate and use social networks (Perceived Enjoyment), and being encouraged to use social networks (Social Influence)

Table 12. ANOVA

1	Regression	1148.374	5	229.675	1418.496	0.000[b]
	Residual	64.604	399	0.162		
	Total	1212.978	404			

a. Dependent Variable: symptoms of depression (Depression)

b. Predictors include: (Constant), trust in social networks to protect your personal information (Trust), perceived ease of use, perceived enjoyment, perceived usefulness of social networks for maintaining relationships with friends and family, and social influence in encouraging the use of social networks

Table 13. Coefficient

Model		Unstandardized Coefficients		Standardized Coefficients	t	Sig.
		B	Std. Error	Beta		
1	(Constant)	−0.531	0.056	-	−9.522	0
	social networks for staying connected with friends and family (Perceived Usefulness)	0.335	0.06	0.302	5.624	0
	navigate and use social networks (Perceived Ease of Use)	−0.035	0.051	−0.028	−0.702	0.483
	use social networks enjoyable (Perceived Enjoyment)	0.309	0.056	0.251	5.523	0
	encourage to use social networks (Social Influence)	0.087	0.068	0.07	1.268	0.205
	trust social networks to protect your personal information (Trust)	0.472	0.034	0.41	13.969	0

a. Dependent Variable: as a means of communication in the future (Behavioral Intention)

b. Users' depression to communicate through social networks is significantly explained by the multiple regression model (R Square = 0.947). The ANOVA results show that the model is significant (p 0.001). "Perceived Usefulness" (Beta = 0.302), "Perceived Enjoyment" (Beta = 0.251), and "Trust" (Beta = 0.410) are the predictors that significantly reduce depression. However, neither "Social Influence" nor "Perceived Ease of Use" substantially affect depression. The constant term indicates that the regression equation has a non-zero intercept since it is negative (−0.531) and statistically significant (p 0.001).

5.6 Correlation Analysis

The correlation matrix reveals that all variables have significant positive relationships. The correlations between "Internet Experience" and "Preferred Social Media" are quite strong (r = 0.971), as are the correlations between "Anxiety" and "Depression" and between "Behavioral Intention" and "R = 0.877". Similarly, to this, there is a substantial correlation between "Preferred Social Media" and "Anxiety" (r = 0.911), "Depression" (r = 0.838), and "Behavioral Intention" (r = 0.910). With respect to "Depression" (r = 0.934) and "Behavioral Intention" (r = 0.945), "Anxiety" has a strong correlation. Last but not least, "Depression" and "Behavioral Intention" have a substantial correlation (r = 0.924). There is a substantial connection between all of the variables, with all correlations being statistically significant at the 0.01 level. "Experience a reduction in anxiety" (r = 0.934) seems to have the greatest impact on "Depression" based on the correlation matrix. This implies that those who use social networks and report lower anxiety levels are also likely to have lower levels of depressive symptoms. Additionally, "As a means of communication in the future" (Behavioral Intention) has a strong positive correlation with depression (r = 0.924), suggesting that people who are more likely to have a higher behavioral intention to communicate with others via social networks in the future may also experience a reduction in depressive symptoms (Table 14).

Table 14. Correlation Analysis

		social networks more often based on your internet experience (Internet Experience)	preferred social media platform for staying connected (Preferred Social Media)	experience a reduction in anxiety (Anxiety)	experience a decrease in depressive symptoms due to using social networks (Depression)	as a means of communication in the future (Behavioral Intention)
social networks more often based on your internet experience (Internet Experience)	Pearson Correlation	1	0.971**	0.932**	0.877**	0.945**
	Sig. (2-tailed)	-	0	0	0	0
	N	405	405	405	405	405
preferred social media platform for staying connected (Preferred Social Media)	Pearson Correlation	0.971**	1	0.911**	0.838**	0.910**
	Sig. (2-tailed)	0	-	0	0	0
	N	405	405	405	405	405
experience a reduction in anxiety (Anxiety)	Pearson Correlation	0.932**	0.911**	1	0.934**	0.945**
	Sig. (2-tailed)	0	0	-	0	0
	N	405	405	405	405	405

(*continued*)

Table 14. (continued)

		social networks more often based on your internet experience (Internet Experience)	preferred social media platform for staying connected (Preferred Social Media)	experience a reduction in anxiety (Anxiety)	experience a decrease in depressive symptoms due to using social networks (Depression)	as a means of communication in the future (Behavioral Intention)
experience a decrease in depressive symptoms due to using social networks (Depression)	Pearson Correlation	0.877^{**}	0.838^{**}	0.934^{**}	1	0.924^{**}
	Sig. (2-tailed)	0	0	0	-	0
	N	405	405	405	405	405
as a means of communication in the future (Behavioral Intention)	Pearson Correlation	0.945^{**}	0.910^{**}	0.945^{**}	0.924^{**}	1
	Sig. (2-tailed)	0	0	0	0	-
	N	405	405	405	405	405

**. Correlation is significant at the 0.01 level (2-tailed).

6 Discussion

According to the study's findings, the data gathered has confirmed and validated each of the assumptions that were put out. All of the variables under investigation have significant positive connections, as shown by the correlation matrix. The relationship between "Internet Experience" and "Preferred Social Media" is significant. The correlations between "Anxiety" and "Depression" as well as "Behavioural Intention" have also been shown to be related. These findings provide greater clarity and knowledge of the interactions between these factors, supporting the overall results derived from the research. On the other hand, there is a substantial connection for the variable "anxiety". It also turns out to be important that "Depression" and "Behavioural Intention" are related. This suggests that the correlation matrix analysis of these variables indicated significant and noteworthy relationships between them. Each component in this context demonstrates a strong relationship with the others. However, it is important to note that the statement "Experience a reduction in anxiety" seems to have the most impact on the component "Depression". Therefore, those who frequently use social networking sites and who also report having lower levels of anxiety are shown to be more likely to have lower levels of depressive symptoms. Furthermore, it's crucial to understand that there is a notable and significant relationship between depressed symptoms and how people want to communicate in the future (this relationship is known as "behavioral intention"). This claim implies that those who are more likely to communicate on social media in the next weeks or months would also likely see a decrease in the intensity of their depression symptoms. This suggests that using social media to communicate with others may enhance people's general mental health by favoring their well-being. The use of social networking sites excessively may have negative effects, including loneliness, increased anxiety, and a higher risk of developing depression, according to recent research, even though these platforms were initially designed to foster connection and enhance well-being generally. But in the case of this research results, it can be observed that social media had several positive influences on depression, such as assisting in reducing anxiety and depression.

7 Conclusion

Objective Linking: The objectives of this study were successfully met since, according to numerous survey and test findings, perceived value, perceived usability, perceived pleasure, and perceived social influence all had a favorable effect on college students' levels of depression. On the other hand, the impact of other significant variables on depression, including behavioral intention, anxiety, social media use, and online experiences, was also discussed.

Limitation and Future Implication: Online questionnaires were used to gather the research's data, although there weren't many of them. More data collection may be the subject of future study, which may be beneficial. The participants, however, were all Indian college students. Students from different nations might be surveyed to get far more varied and useful data for the study.

Conclusion: This paper looked at the factors that affect depression among Indian college students. The investigation into the effects of several aspects, including perceived easiness, perceived usefulness, and many more, on depression is all favorable. The article also looks at the significant factors that impact college students' mental health, focusing on factors related to depression, such as anxiety, FOMO, and cyberbullying. This research also identifies these causes and offers practical suggestions, like exercising, for lowering or eliminating the depression issue among Indian college students.

Recommendations: It highly advises regular exercise as a powerful strategy for lowering anxiety and depressive symptoms. This advice is based on the knowledge that physical exercise significantly enhances mental health. This is also supported by a survey result conducted by Minhas (2023b) reports that approximately 59 per cent of respondents in the 55 and older age bracket have recently started a regular exercise regimen as a strategy to enhance their mental well-being, according to a recent Rakuten Insight survey conducted in India in May 2022. The poll also showed that various widely used strategies are used to promote mental well-being, including bettering sleep patterns and practicing mindfulness and meditation.

Various student support groups will be organized as those will significantly help reduce such issues. This is also supported by research by Mirza et al. (2021), where it is recommended that adolescents should have a comprehensive understanding of these problems and receive psychiatric counselling during their initial years of schooling. The student support group should provide assistance to help them address and mitigate the associated challenges that could potentially jeopardize their future academic and professional success.

8 Declaration

The authors declare that they have not used any type of generative artificial intelligence for the writing of this manuscript, nor for the creation of images, graphics, tables, or their corresponding captions.

References

Bisen, S.S., Deshpande, Y.: Prevalence, predictors, psychological correlates of internet addiction among college students in India: a comprehensive study. Anatolian J. Psychiatry/Anadolu Psikiyatri Dergisi, 21(2) (2020)

Bolodeoku, P.B., Igbinoba, E., Salau, P.O., Chukwudi, C.K., Idia, S.E.: Perceived usefulness of technology and multiple salient outcomes: the improbable case of oil and gas workers. Heliyon **8**(4) (2022)

Cheng, L., Guo, R., Silva, Y., Hall, D., Liu, H.: Hierarchical attention networks for cyberbullying detection on the Instagram social network. In: Proceedings of the 2019 SIAM International Conference on Data Mining, pp. 235–243 (2019). Society for Industrial and Applied Mathematics.

MA Fabris D Marengo C Longobardi M Settanni 2020 Investigating the links between fear of missing out, social media addiction, and emotional symptoms in adolescence: the role of stress associated with neglect and negative reactions on social media Addict. Behav. 106 106364

R Ferdianto 2022 The role of perceived usefulness and perceived ease of use in increasing repurchase intention in the era of the Covid-19 pandemic Res. Horizon 2 2 313 329

Firth-Cozens, J.: A perspective on stress and depression. In: Understanding Doctors' Performance, pp. 22–37. CRC Press (2023)

Goel, A., Gupta, L.: Social media in the times of COVID-19. JCR: J. Clin. Rheumatol. **26**(6), 220–223 (2020). https://doi.org/10.1097/rhu.0000000000001508

Jiang, S., Ngien, A.: The effects of Instagram use, social comparison, and self-esteem on social anxiety: a survey study in Singapore. Soc. Media+ Soc. **6**(2), 2056305120912488 (2020)

C Kraus B Kadriu R Lanzenberger CA Zarate Jr S Kasper 2019 Prognosis and improved outcomes in major depression: a review Transl. Psychiatry 9 1 127

Minhas, A.: India: people feeling more stressed by age 2022. Statista (2023a). https://www.statista.com/statistics/1320246/india-people-feeling-more-stressed-by-age/. Accessed 3 Aug 2023

Minhas, A.: India: practices undertaken to improve mental wellness by age (2022). Statista. https://www.statista.com/statistics/1322163/india-practices-undertaken-to-improve-mental-wellness-by-age/. Accessed 3 Aug 2023.

Mirza, A.A., Baig, M., Beyari, G.M., Halawani, M.A., Mirza, A.A.: Depression and anxiety among medical students: a brief overview. In: Advances in Medical Education and Practice, pp.393–398 (2021)

News18: Cases of depression, social media addiction on the rise among youth during pandemic, say docs. News18. https://www.news18.com/news/india/cases-of-depression-social-media-addiction-on-the-rise-among-youth-during-pandemic-say-docs-4153883.html. Accessed 3 Aug 2023

Patil, H.P., Atique, M.: Sentiment analysis for social media: a survey. In: 2015 2nd International Conference on Information Science and Security (ICISS), pp. 1–4. IEEE, December 2015

HP Patil M Atique 2020 CDNB: CAVIAR-dragonfly optimization with naive Bayes for the sentiment and affect analysis in social media Big Data 8 2 107 124

Paykel, E.S.: Basic concepts of depression. Dialogues Clin. Neurosci. **10**(3), 279–289 (2022). https://doi.org/10.31887/dcns.2008.10.3/espaykel

E Seidl 2020 Response to ostracism in patients with chronic depression, episodic depression and borderline personality disorder a study using Cyberball J. Affect. Disord. 260 254 262

N Singh N Sinha FJ Liébana-Cabanillas 2020 Determining factors in the adoption and recommendation of mobile wallet services in India: analysis of the effect of innovativeness, stress to use and social influence Int. J. Inf. Manage. 50 191 205

The Economic Times: Social media addiction turning into a mental health challenge. The Economic Times (2022). https://economictimes.indiatimes.com/news/india/social-media-addiction-turning-into-a-mental-health-challenge/articleshow/95159021.cms?from=mdr

Towards a Unified Framework of Digital Competencies on e-Health: A Systematic Review of Current Approaches and Challenges

Uxía Regueira[1] (iD), Virginia Rodés-Paragarino[1 (✉)] (iD), and Viola Davini[2] (iD)

[1] Tecnologico de Monterrey, Institute for the Future of Education, Europe (IFE Europe), 48014 Bilbao, Spain
`virginia.rodes@ifeeurope.es`
[2] Research Center for Generative Communication, 50122 Florence, Italy

Abstract. Digital transformation has profoundly impacted the healthcare sector, necessitating the reformulation of curricula in health professions. The EUpro-Health 2021–2027 plan underscores the importance of strengthening digital competencies among professionals. This systematic review analyzes the existing digital competence frameworks and highlights the lack of a specific European framework for the health sector. The findings suggest the need for a unified approach that addresses the current demands of digital competence in healthcare and facilitates a curricular reform aligned with emerging technological needs.

Keywords: Digital Competencies · Digital Skills · E-Health Educational Innovation · Higher Education

1 Introduction

Digital transformation has revolutionized virtually all aspects of contemporary society, and the healthcare sector is no exception. This change encompasses everything from modifying professional practice to transforming the citizenry that the sector serves. To respond to these changes, it has become imperative to reformulate the curricula of health-related degrees, aligning them with a constantly evolving socio-health and technological context.

In this context, the European Union has promoted initiatives such as the EUproHealth 2021–2027 plan, which aims to "strengthen health data, digital tools and services, and the digital transformation of healthcare" [1]. This strategic framework highlights the urgent need to train healthcare professionals in digital competencies (DC), not only to improve their technical skills and incorporate technological advances into clinical practice but also to adapt to an ever-changing citizenry.

To respond to this need, initiatives have emerged at both the European and national levels (Spain), such as the digital competence frameworks promoted by the NHS in the United Kingdom [2] and the COMPDIG_Salu project in Catalonia [3]. Additionally, validated tools such as Digi-HealthCom, e-HEALS, and the Digital Health Literacy

A. K. Somani et al. (Eds.): ICNCS 2025, CCIS 2718, pp. 105–114, 2026.
https://doi.org/10.1007/978-3-032-12544-6_8

Instrument [4] have been created to measure competence development. However, the lack of consensus around a common framework for digital competencies in the health-care sector, akin to what exists in the educational field, represents a significant challenge for creating curricula adapted to current needs. This gap underscores the need for an integrated and unified approach that includes perspectives from health, education, communication, and engineering to address the challenges of the digital age.

This document presents a systematic review of the literature on digital competencies in the healthcare sector, with the aim of identifying similarities and differences in current proposals and analyzing the challenges these frameworks face. Through this review, the objective is to contribute to the advancement towards a research-based common framework that enables the training of better-prepared healthcare professionals to face the challenges of an increasingly digitalized environment.

2 Methodology

To conduct this systematic review, the initial phases of the PRISMA 2020 statement [5] were adopted. This decision follows current trends in bibliographic review in academia. However, it is important to consider that this guide originates from the healthcare field and aims to evaluate the effects of its results [5], whereas this work does not intend to conduct meta-analysis and statistical synthesis. Therefore, only those items from the checklist [5] are followed that allow for documenting the search strategy, selection, registration, characterization of studies, and individual results.

In accordance with item 5 of the PRISMA 2020 checklist regarding eligibility criteria [5], texts written in English or Spanish, published between 2019 and 2024, and appearing as scientific articles in peer-reviewed journals were included. Following item 6, the selected sources were: SCOPUS, Web of Science (WOS), and IEEE. According to item 7 (Search Strategies) [5], terms were selected that—through their combination—allow for the description of the topic: digital competence, digital skills, literacy, and health professional. Additionally, the limits facilitated by the databases were included, which allow for the mechanization of inclusion criteria: publication date, language of the text, and type of publication. Based on this combination, the search equations documented in Table 1 were configured.

From this search, an initial volume of 30 articles was obtained. For filtering and selection, the exclusion criteria outlined in Table 2 were established in accordance with item 8 of the PRISMA 2020 checklist [5].

In these criteria, the repetition of articles is considered, resulting from returns under different search equations as well as indexing in various databases. Non-empirical articles that do not provide results accounting for the state of the question are excluded. Finally, articles that do not fit the topic are excluded in two phases: non-adequacy to the title or abstract, and non-adequacy after reading the full corpus.

The complete data from each search result is downloaded in BibTex format and uploaded to Zotero for easy access, organization, and management. In parallel, these results are recorded in an Excel spreadsheet. This spreadsheet is used to assign a code to each search result—that allows for naming each article and linking it to the database from which it was extracted—and to record each of the criteria applied for its selection or

Table 1. Registration of the search

Database	Date	Search equation
Scopus	4/10	[("digital competence" OR "digital skills") AND "health professional"] + limit to: range 2019–2024, article, english or spanish
WOS	4/10	("digital competence" OR "digital skills") AND "health professional"
IEEE Explore	4/10	("digital competence" OR "digital skills") AND "health professional") + limit to: range 2019–2024, article
Total	30	

Table 2. Exclusion criteria

EC	Exclusion criteria
E.C.1	Repeated
E.C.2	Non-empirical article
E.C.3	The title and summary are not appropriate to the subject matter
E.C.4	The body of the article is not appropriate to the topic
E.C.1	Repeated

exclusion. These codes are formed by combining the first three letters of the source name or its acronym with the number of the article in the search results sorted in descending order (e.g., WOS01). According to the records in the Excel spreadsheet, which are summarized in the flowchart in Fig. 1, a final corpus of 14 articles is obtained.

The final corpus was qualitatively analyzed to identify patterns, trends, and deficiencies in the conceptual approach to digital competence in the healthcare sector.

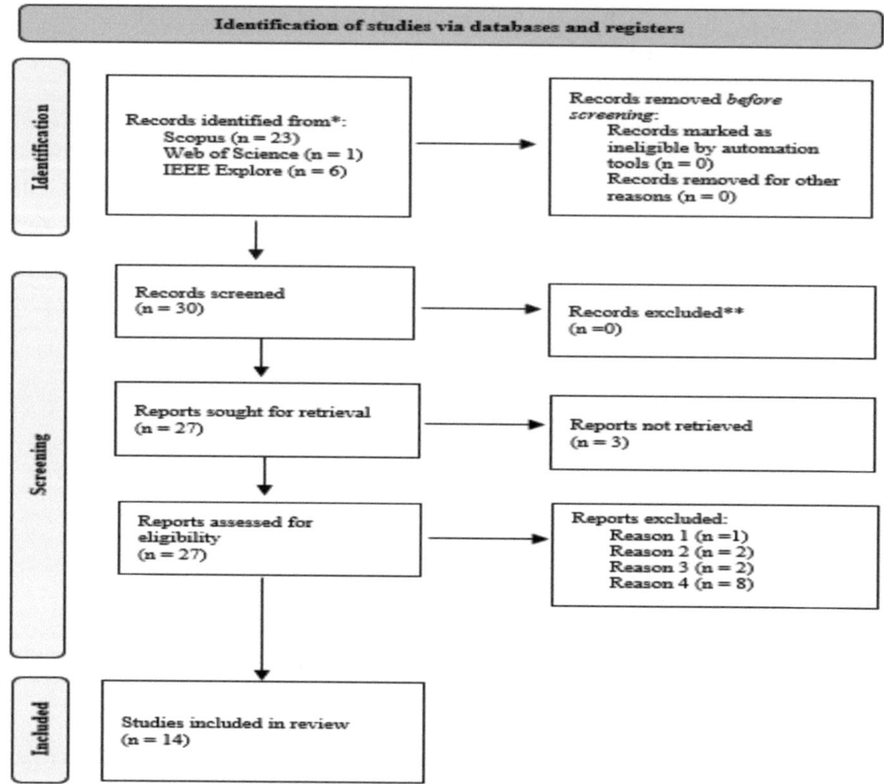

Fig. 1. Prisma 2020 Flow Diagram for Systematic Reviews. Source: template proposed by Page et al. (2020) for illustrating the article selection process. Its use under citation is acknowledged at http://www.prisma-statement.org/PRISMAStatement/CitingAndUsingPRISMA.aspx

3 Results

In the resulting corpus, the predominant texts are written from Spain (4), Germany (2), and Finland (2) (Fig. 2), by authors from up to 10 different disciplines, among which medicine (10), nursing (3), information management (3), and education (3) stand out (Fig. 3). Disciplines such as computer science or engineering appear in a single article as co-authors.

The majority of the corpus addresses digital competence in a comprehensive sense for healthcare practice; however, a significant portion is divided into the specific approach of competence development in the informational area [6, 7], communicational area [8], for online learning [9, 10], instrumental and operational management for the practice of telemedicine [11–14], and the digital health of professionals in the field [15].

Only one of the articles aims to construct a digital competence measurement instrument; the majority focus on measuring self-perceived performance [14, 16, 17] or third-party perceptions [9, 10] and the implementation of workshops for competence development [6, 7, 13, 18–20].

Fig. 2. Countries Where the Authors' Affiliation is Located

It is noteworthy that, although 9 of the articles in the corpus have healthcare personnel as their broad target population, a portion of the corpus focuses on teachers and students in higher education within health-related disciplines. These articles address digital competence by directing reflection towards the curricular design of academic programs and how it responds to the demands of societal transformation.

3.1 Digital Competence Frameworks

The majority of the corpus does not identify and delimit a conceptual framework within which to situate the proposal; among those that do identify one, the use of Digcomp [21–23] stands out, all of which are from the European context, within which DigCompEdu [24] is mentioned. Marginally, the specific Finnish context framework MEDigi [16], eHLF [13], and an unreferenced framework [17] are also mentioned (Table 3).

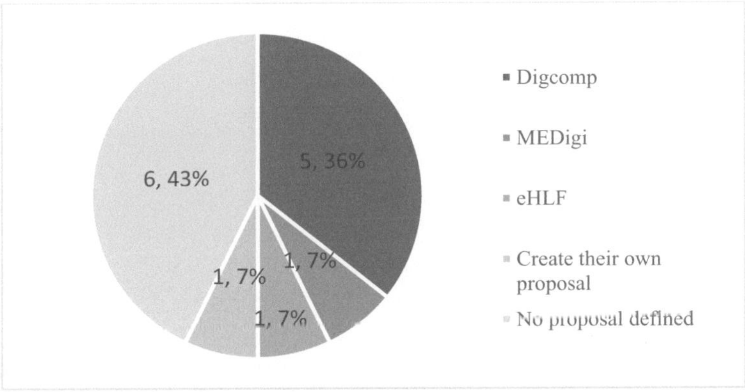

Fig. 3. Conceptual Frameworks of DC

Table 3. Digital Competence Frameworks

	Digital Competence Frameworks	
Framework	**Digcomp / DigcompEdu**	**MEDigi**
Origin	Europe	Finland
Target	General Citizenship	Health Professionals (eHealth)
Dimensions	(1) Information and Digital Literacy: Competencies related to the search, management, evaluation, and critical use of information and data in digital environments (2) Communication and Collaboration: Skills for interacting, communicating, and collaborating through digital tools (3) Digital Content Creation: Capacity to develop new and original content, as well as adapt and modify existing digital content (4) Security: Focus on the protection of devices, data, and privacy, including digital well-being. It encompasses topics such as personal data protection, digital risk management, and understanding the potential impacts of digital technologies on health (5) Problem Solving: Skills to identify, evaluate, and resolve problems in digital environments	(1) Electronic Health Records (EHR) Systems (2) Electronic Databases and Clinical Decision Support Systems (3) National Health Information Exchange Services (4) Information Systems and Technologies Integrated into the Healthcare System (5) Information Security and Data Privacy (6) Generation and Utilization of Patient and Health Data (7) Interaction in a Digital Environment (8) Big Data in Medicine and Healthcare (9) Health Technology Assessment (10) Megatrends in Digital Healthcare (11) Development, Research, and Innovations (12) Medical Technology
	Digital Competence Frameworks	
Framework	**eHLF**	**Burgos et al. [17]**
Origin	Academy	Academy
Target	Health Professionals (eHealth)	Nursing

(*continued*)

Table 3. (continued)

	Digital Competence Frameworks	
Dimensions	(1) Information and Digital Literacy: Competencies related to the search, management, evaluation, and critical use of information and data in digital environments (2) Communication and Collaboration: Skills for interacting, communicating, and collaborating through digital tools (3) Digital Content Creation: Capacity to develop new and original content, as well as adapt and modify existing digital content (4) Security: Focus on the protection of devices, data, and privacy, including digital well-being. It encompasses topics such as personal data protection, digital risk management, and understanding the potential impacts of digital technologies on health (5) Problem Solving: Skills to identify, evaluate, and resolve problems in digital environments	(1) Electronic Health Records (EHR) Systems (2) Electronic Databases and Clinical Decision Support Systems (3) National Health Information Exchange Services (4) Information Systems and Technologies Integrated into the Healthcare System (5) Information Security and Data Privacy (6) Generation and Utilization of Patient and Health Data (7) Interaction in a Digital Environment (8) Big Data in Medicine and Healthcare (9) Health Technology Assessment (10) Megatrends in Digital Healthcare (11) Development, Research, and Innovations (12) Medical Technology

3.2 Limitations and Opportunities of the Frameworks

The DigComp [21–23] framework, although widely used, presents limitations in addressing specific issues within the healthcare sector. Its focus is highlighted in studies that explore digital competence (DC) in students, where the ability to manage digital tools for mediating learning situations is valued. However, it does not sufficiently consider the necessary preparation for performing professional functions in a hybrid society. Specifically, the corpus indicates that the healthcare sector faces unique challenges related to patient privacy protection, data management ethics, the use of artificial intelligence for diagnosis, and communication with patients immersed in the phenomenon of information overload [4], among others. These challenges are inherently linked to the intersection of the healthcare field and disciplines that converge in technological design and data processing, which are far removed from the regular exercise of general citizenship. DigComp [21–23] is designed as a training framework for exercising such citizenship, and while it can act as a reference, it does not comprehensively address the competencies required for specific professional performance, especially those that require a deep understanding of the healthcare domain and the technologies that mediate this practice.

In this context, several risks arise:

- Limitations of the framework to the health area for citizens: Studies that use DigComp as a reference framework tend to focus on measuring competencies for personal digital health management [4], rather than specialized professional practice and the relationship with a patient subject or research object.
- Limitations on performance as a student or teacher: Similarly, to what has already been mentioned, the ability to learn or teach in a hybrid context, where digital technologies play a fundamental role in these processes, is valued [10]. From this perspective, the revision of curricula is proposed, but the results indicate that subjects perceive themselves as competent in these processes, not in those related to professional practice [14, 20].

On the other hand, frameworks specifically developed for the healthcare sector partially address these deficiencies. Special emphasis is placed on the instrumental management of specific technologies for medical practice, something that DigComp [21–23] does not adequately address from the educational field and for which it has been widely criticized, as it assumes basic instrumental management. These frameworks recognize the need for digital competencies that enable healthcare professionals not only to adapt to technological tools but also to use them for conducting research, analyzing data, and managing clinical contexts effectively in a digitized environment. However, these conceptual frameworks do not offer well-defined and clear dimensions that allow for their concretization into clearly measurable sub-competencies. At the same time, due to the specificity of their focus and the detachment from a global digital citizenship approach, there is a risk of limiting the view to telemedicine and the implementation of technological solutions in specific tasks. Particularly in the management of software and compliance with ethical codes and legislative frameworks, without considering the broader transformations of professional practice in health or the redefinition of the notion of ethics itself, as addressed in the article Caeiros et al. [8] situated in digital communication. An important aspect of digital competence in healthcare that remains underemphasized in existing frameworks is the role of communicative skills. Beyond technical proficiency, healthcare professionals require advanced communication capabilities to ensure effective interaction with patients and colleagues in increasingly digital environments.

4 Conclusions

In conclusion, the study results show a predominant adoption of the DigComp [21–23] educational frameworks in Spanish and European contexts, rather than the development of a specific framework for the healthcare sector. This trend suggests a moderate adaptation of general digital competence frameworks, which may not adequately respond to the specific needs of the e-Health domain. Based on the findings, it is proposed that a consensus-based competency framework be created from the existing scientific production, identifying gaps that need to be addressed through research efforts. To this end, it is crucial to develop a holistic framework that can take DigComp as a reference but be repositioned through an interdisciplinary dialogue in concrete professional practice and the challenges of its time.

The need to rethink curricula is evident, placing digital competencies in professional practice rather than civic practice, directly addressing the gap between the plan designed from the educational field and the healthcare field. Finally, there is an emerging concern around data handling and processing, such as big data, which demands a specialized dialogue about the technological challenges these data impose. This underscores the importance of including the technological field in the discussion and development of an appropriate competency framework for e-Health.

Acknowledgements. The authors wish to acknowledge the financial support of the Writing Lab, Institute for the Future of Education, Tecnologico de Monterrey.

Declaration. The authors declare that they have not used any type of generative artificial intelligence for the writing of this manuscript, nor for the creation of images, graphics, tables, or their corresponding.

References

1. European Commission: Objectives of the EU4Health programme. Publications Office of the European Union (2021). https://health.ec.europa.eu/document/download/26327adc-de3e-4e66-b93a-5ec1c8ef48ab_en?filename=eu4health-2021-2027_2022-work-prog_en.pdf
2. NHS England: Profession and Service Specific Digital Capabilities Frameworks (2020). https://tinyurl.com/2hx9d3vy
3. Guitert, M., Romeu, T., Hernández, E., Saigí, F.: Mapa de Competències Digitals per als professionals de Salut (2024). https://mapa-compdig-salut.uoc.edu/
4. Karvouniari, A., et al.: Translation and validation of digital competence indicators in Greek for health professionals: a cross-sectional study. Healthcare **12**, 1370 (2024). https://doi.org/10.3390/healthcare12141370
5. Page, M.J., et al.: The PRISMA 2020 statement: an updated guideline for reporting systematic reviews. BMJ **372**(71) (2021). https://doi.org/10.1136/bmj.n71
6. Fernández Luque, A.M.: On-the-job digital competence training for health professionals. Revista Cubana de Información en Ciencias de la Salud **30**(2), e1322 (2019)
7. Terry, J., Davies, A., Williams, C., Tait, S., Condon, L.: Improving the digital literacy competence of nursing and midwifery students: a qualitative study of the experiences of NICE student champions. Nurse Educ. Pract. **34**, 192–199 (2019). https://doi.org/10.1016/j.nepr.2018.11.016
8. Caeiros, P., Pita Ferreira, P., Chen-Xu, J., Francisco, R., Telo de Arriaga, M.: From health communication to health literacy: a comprehensive analysis of relevance and strategies. Public Health **42**(2), 159–164 (2024). https://doi.org/10.1159/000537870
9. Byungura, J.C., Nyiringango, G., Fors, U., Forsberg, E., Tumusiime, D.K.: Online learning for continuous professional development of healthcare workers: an exploratory study on perceptions of healthcare managers in Rwanda. BMC Med. Educ. **22**, 851 (2022). https://doi.org/10.1186/s12909-022-03938-y
10. Mensonen, M., Pramila-Savukoski, S., Mikkonen, K., Törmänen, T., Juntunen, J., Kuivila, H.M.: The experiences of social and health care and health sciences educators of implementing hybrid teaching in higher education: a qualitative study. Nurse Educ. Today **133**, 106079 (2024). https://doi.org/10.1016/j.nedt.2023.106079
11. Contreras, P.J., Castillo-Narro, M., Huerta-Mercado, J., Cuba-Fuentes, M.S.: Programa de Teleconsulta Docente: percepciones de profesores y alumnos de una facultad de medicina peruana. Acta Med Peru **39**(2), 138–150 (2022). https://doi.org/10.35663/amp.2022.392.2243
12. Esposito, S., et al.: Information and training on the use of telemedicine in pediatric population: consensus document of the Italian society of telemedicine (SIT). J. Pers. Med. **13**, 314 (2023). https://doi.org/10.3390/jpm13020314

13. Kayser, L., et al.: Health professionals' eHealth literacy and system experience before and 3 months after the implementation of an electronic health record system: longitudinal study. JMIR Hum. Fact. **9**(2), e29780 (2022). https://doi.org/10.2196/29780

14. Machleid, F., et al.: Perceptions of digital health education among European medical students: mixed methods survey. J. Med. Internet **22**(8), e19827 (2020). https://doi.org/10.2196/19827

15. Golz, C., Peter, K.A., Müller, T.J., Mutschler, J., Zwakhalen, S.M.G., Hahn, S.: Technostress and digital competence among health professionals in Swiss psychiatric hospitals: cross-sectional study. JMIR Ment Health **8**(11), e31408 (2021). https://doi.org/10.2196/31408

16. Veikkolainen, P., Tuovinen, T., Jarva, E., Tuomikoski, A.M., Männistö, M., Pääkkönen, J.: eHealth competence building for future doctors and nurses – attitudes and capabilities. Int. J. Med. Inform. **169**, 104912 (2022). https://doi.org/10.1016/j.ijmedinf.2022.104912

17. Burgos, D., López-Serrano, A., Palmisano, S., Timmins, F., Connolly, M.: Digital competencies for nurses: tools for responding to spiritual care needs. Healthcare **10**, 1966 (2022). https://doi.org/10.3390/healthcare10101966

18. Kraft, B., Kuscher, T., Zawatzki, S., Hofstetter, S., Jahn, P.: Evaluation of the Continuing Education Training 'Beratende für Digitale Gesundheitsversorgung' ('Consultant for Digital Healthcare'). JMIR **13**, 57860 (2024). https://doi.org/10.2196/57860

19. Fernández Luque, A.M., Ramirez-Montoya, M.S.: Health professionals' competencies in the framework of complexity: digital training model for education 4.0. Revista Española de Documentación Científica **47**(2), 383 (2024). https://doi.org/10.3989/redc.2024.2.1470

20. Meng Cham, K., Edwards, M.L., Kruesi, L., Celeste, T., Hennessey, T.: Digital preferences and perceptions of students in health professional courses at a leading Australian university: a baseline for improving digital skills and competencies in health graduates. Australas. J. Educ. Technol. **38**(1), 69–86 (2022). https://doi.org/10.14742/ajet.6622

21. Ferrari, A.: DIGCOMP: a framework for developing and understanding digital competence in Europe. Publications Office of the European Union (2013). https://doi.org/10.2788/52966

22. Carretero, S., Vuorikari, R., Punie, Y.: DigComp 2.1: the digital competence framework for citizens with eight proficiency levels and examples of use. Publications Office of the European Union (2017). https://doi.org/10.2760/38842

23. Vuorikari, R., Kluzer, S., Punie, Y.: DigComp 2.2: the digital competence framework for citizens. Publications Office of the European Union (2022). https://doi.org/10.2760/115376

24. Redecker, C., Punie, Y.: Digital competence framework for educators. Joint Research Centre, European Commission (2020). https://joint-research-centre.ec.europa.eu/digcompedu/digcompedu-framework_en

Author Index